Helping Children See Jesus

BEING JESUS' DISCIPLE
A Family Worship Study on the Gospel of Mark

Illustrators: Bethany Moy, Olivia Moy   Page Layout: Lindsay Hess
Author: Jeffrey Kilcup
Hymn Typeset Credit: Grace Music, Celebrating Grace Inc

© 2021 Bible Visuals International
PO Box 153, Akron, PA 17501-0153
Phone: (717) 859-1131
www.biblevisuals.org
ISBN 978-1-64104-150-8

All rights reserved. No part of this publication may be reproduced, stored in a retrieval system or transmitted in any form by any means, electronic, mechanical, photocopy, recording or otherwise, without the prior permission of the publisher, except as provided by USA copyright law.

READ   TALK   PRAY   SING

Special thanks to Josh Scherrer and William Shaul for providing editorial feedback for this volume.

BVI is a 501(c)(3) charity organization. We rely on the support of ministry partners like you to help us in our mission of Helping Children See Jesus. If you would like to learn more, please visit biblevisuals.org.

What can my family learn through this Bible study?

Your family will be encouraged to read God's Word together and worship Him in the beauty of His holiness

You will understand the themes and outline of an entire book of the Bible

Your family will learn how to study the Bible

You will learn from the Bible in an ongoing family conversation

Pointers for Parents

Listen patiently. Your children's answers are windows into their young hearts. Each discussion is a chance to understand the children you are discipling for Christ.

Use your family Bible. The Bible text is not provided to you for a reason - so that family members open their own Bibles together.

Take breaks. It may be helpful to take a break for a few days or even a week. The idea is to learn, not follow a rigid system or plan.

Help your kids make connections. While there are many moralistic devotional books for children, this Bible study focuses on observation and the author's intent. In this study you will tackle the text section-by-section to underscore the authority of the Bible itself, skipping nothing.

Grow. Allow God to teach/guide/grow *you* in the process of discipling your children.

How do we use this Bible study?

Read

In this section, read the Bible passage aloud as a family. Consider changing who reads each passage, or alternate every couple of verses. Keep it fresh!

Talk

This section is not intended to be exhaustive or exhausting. Keep the study moving unless you see the need to slow down for tender hearts that are seeking God.

This section aims to draw out themes or details that might be easily overlooked in a cursory reading.

Pray

The prayer-from-the-heart section gives an opportunity for heart-application, encouraging your family to consider: "what should be my heart attitude about this study?"

Sing

Singing in your home, whatever quality it may have, communicates to the next generation that 1) this faith is real, and 2) it is real *to me*. Joyful singing of gospel truth connects scripture to the heart and helps children remember the truth they have been taught.

Each daily suggested hymn in the Family Worship Study is included in the back of this volume with the melody line and chords for use of a family instrument. If you do not know a song, simply read the poetry aloud together!

 ### Extra Time / Activities

Sometimes you may find there is extra time or you want to help your children compare a study's theme with other passages of the Bible. Many of the studies include activities and further study to clarify the truths discussed that day.

Study Length

About 15-20 minutes should be enough time to **Read** the passage, **Talk** it through, **Pray** together, and **Sing** a few verses from the song for that study.

You know your children. Pace each study to minister to their hearts and develop an awe for God and His Word.

Outline for the Gospel of Mark

Part 1: Mark chapters 1 - 9

    Being God's Servant: Jesus in Galilee

    "What does it mean to be a disciple?"

Part 2: Mark chapters 9 - 16

    The Suffering Servant: Jesus to Jerusalem

    "What did Jesus do to obey God?"

Mark's Gospel
STUDY #1

Following Jesus Means Being a Servant

📖 **Read:** Mark 10:42-45

💬 **Talk:**

1. Each book of the Bible has a theme or big idea that the author (or writer) wanted everyone who read the book to understand. The theme of the Gospel of Mark is "Being Jesus' Disciple". The goal of this study book is to help our family understand what it really means to be Jesus' disciple and follower.

2. What does it mean to be "the boss?" *(makes decisions, important person)*

3. From verse 42, how does a selfish leader (or boss) act? *(proud, bossy, selfish)*

4. What does it mean to be a servant in your attitude? *(humble, thoughtful, not selfish)*

5. As Jesus is talking to his disciples in verses 43 & 44, who is considered important in Jesus' opinion? *(servants)*

6. The book of Mark has another theme, or big idea, that is being written about. Mark explains that Jesus is God's servant. What are the two reasons Jesus gives in verse 45 for him coming to earth? *(Jesus came to serve and to give his life to rescue many people)* The book of Mark will help us discover how Jesus did both of those things.

7. In the Bible, a person who follows Jesus and learns from Jesus is a "disciple." In this passage, we learn that following Jesus means being like a servant more than being the boss.

8. What would being a servant look like in your home? For a parent? For a child? *(parents can be both authority and servant at the same time, ask forgiveness after losing temper, etc; children can obey humbly, help out without being asked, etc.)*

❤️ **Pray:** Father, thank you for sending Jesus to earth. He was not bossy or selfish, but he served other people and helped them to know You better. As we study the book of Mark, help us to learn how Jesus was a servant and how we can be like him. Father, we confess that our hearts are selfish and we try to be the boss. Help us be more like Jesus today and serve other people instead of wanting them to serve us. Thank you for all the things we will learn while we study Mark.

🎵 **Sing:** Sing "Trust and Obey" together in response to what you have read today. (pg 111)

⇒ EXTRA TIME? ⇐

Think of a chore or task that your family has to do every day or week. Pick a chore that no one particularly loves. *(cleaning the bathroom, washing dishes, feeding animals, etc)* How can your family show love to each other and serve one another with that task?

Mark's Gospel
STUDY #2

True Disciples Follow and Obey

📖 **Read:** Mark 1:1-1:13

💬 **Talk:**

1. From verse 1 (v1), what is the book of Mark about? *(the gospel of Jesus Christ)*

2. Why is it important that Jesus is called "the Son of God" here at the beginning of Mark? *(Giving Jesus this title helps us understand Jesus' special relationship to God... He is God!)*

3. Read vs2-8 again. Cross reference (look up and compare) them with Malachi 3:1 and Isaiah 40:3. How is John the Baptist described in the passage for today? *(review clothing and diet)* Does he seem like a strange messenger? If you were an important and powerful person, how would you like your messenger to dress and live?

4. Read v4 and v9. The Bible tells us Jesus was sinless (1 John 3:5), yet he was baptized by John. What is repentance? *(choosing obedience to God by turning away from sin)* Did Jesus need to repent of sin? *(No)* Then why did Jesus go to be baptized? *(to obey God / show His choice to follow God / leave us an example of obedience)*

5. What happened right after Jesus' baptism? (hint: vs12-13) *(Jesus goes to the desert and is tempted by Satan)* Jesus never sinned. He always pleased God, by doing right *(baptism)* and refusing to do wrong *(that is, refusing to sin when tempted to do wrong)*.

6. Jesus shows us how God's servant obeys. What were the two examples Mark gives us to prove that Jesus obeyed? *(Jesus' baptism and temptation)*

7. The story of Jesus in the book of Mark moves very quickly and a lot happens in the first thirteen sentences! Mark has two goals in his book, that everyone who reads it would first know who Jesus is, and second know what it means to be a true disciple (or follower) of Jesus.

❤️ **Pray:** Father, thank you for sending Jesus, your Son, to earth. Jesus obeyed you, and we want to obey as well. Jesus refused to disobey you when he was tempted, and we want to please you too. Whatever you ask us to do in your Word, help us follow and obey.

🎵 **Sing:** Sing "Trust and Obey" in response to what you have read today! (pg 111)

⇒ **EXTRA TIME?** ⇐

Expand on John's clothing and how the Jewish mind would think back to Elijah the Tishbite (and the account where a king recognizes Elijah by the description of his clothing). The Point: John's clothing meant something to the original audience, kind of like someone humming a movie theme song today: it brings a picture, idea, or feeling to mind. John's clothing reminded people of Elijah.

Mark's Gospel
— STUDY #3 —

Jesus' Fame Grows

📖 **Read:** Mark 1:14-1:34

💬 **Talk:**

1. This section tells us how Jesus called disciples, healed people, and taught his followers. In v14, who was put in prison? *(John the Baptist)*

2. When the Bible repeats words, it is usually on purpose. How many times does the word "immediately" occur in Mark chapter one? *(depending on translation, 8 times)* Mark also has many action-phrases like "as soon as". Pay attention! While you study this book, see how many times you can find words and phrases like these.

3. How many men did Jesus tell to follow him in v16-20? *(four)* What was their job? *(fishermen)*

4. When Jesus called to the fishermen, did they wait a while or pack a lunch first? *(no)* What word tells us they didn't delay or get distracted? *(immediately)* Yes! When God's Word tells us how to obey, should we delay or make excuses? *(no!)*

5. Do you know what an "unclean spirit" is? (v23) *(someone who has been demon-possessed and does evil)* Did the demon know who Jesus is? *(yes, v24)* Did the people seem to understand who Jesus is? *(no, they were surprised)*

6. In v22 and v27 there are words that start with the letter "A". What are these words? *(authority and astonished/amazed)* Why do you think people were amazed that Jesus spoke with authority? *(they hadn't heard anyone else teach like him or command demons what to do)*

7. Why does Jesus have authority over demons? *(because He is God)*

8. What else did Jesus do to show his authority in vs31-32? *(healed Peter's mom)* We see that Jesus has authority over spirits **and** sickness too.

9. Read v28 and v33 - What happened as people began to talk about Jesus and what he was doing? *(fame spread and crowds grew)*

❤️ **Pray:** God, you have all the authority in the universe because you made it. You created planets and galaxies, people and flowers. We want to live under your authority, and not try to rule our own lives. When you tell us how we should follow you and obey, help us to be like the disciples, who immediately left to follow Jesus.

🎵 **Sing:** Sing "I Sing the Mighty Power of God" and remember how Jesus has power over everything. (pg 105)

⇒ EXTRA TIME? ⇐
Read the passage again and pay attention to the word "immediately" and other action-phrases like "as soon as". When you read them, say "Action!" out loud so that everyone studying with you notices the action words too. Continue to point out these words. Make a game of it as you read the book of Mark together in the weeks ahead!

Mark's Gospel
— STUDY #4 —

First Things First

📖 **Read:** Mark 1:35-45

💬 **Talk:**

1. From v35, what did Jesus do to prepare for the day? *[went alone to pray]* What were some of the important things Jesus did during the day? *[preach and heal people]*

2. Before Jesus did mighty things FOR God, he made sure he was walking closely WITH God. Why do you think it is important to pray to God at the beginning of the day? *[answers will vary]* It's important to do the most important things first!

3. Who comes to Jesus in v40? *[a leper]* What does he believe Jesus can do for him? *[heal him of his incurable disease]* In Bible times, there was no medicine to treat leprosy. But Jesus could!

4. What was Jesus' emotion toward this man? (v41) *[He had pity]*

5. The book of Mark is a book of action! If you did the "Extra Time" from Study 3, you noticed an action word in v42. What is it? *[immediately]*

6. In Bible times, sick people went to the Israelite priests to prove they were 'clean' once they got better. Jesus told this man to go to the priests quietly so that the priests would have proof of Who Jesus is - God's servant and Messiah.

7. Jesus had wanted to go out TO people (v38), but because the leper disobeyed and loudly told everyone about Jesus, he couldn't do that. Verse 45 tells us that people came to Jesus instead.

8. Was it wrong for the man to disobey Jesus? *[yes]* Do you think his actions ended up ruining Jesus' ministry? *[no, Jesus followed God's will perfectly and people can't mess that up]* Jesus preached the gospel to serve and save us. Before we can be a servant like Jesus, we need to be served *by* Jesus through the gospel!

❤️ **Pray:** Father, Jesus gave us a good example to follow. We will talk with You often in prayer, because we cannot do Your will without Your help. While the leper didn't honor Jesus' command, help us to honor Your Word even when we don't understand Your commands completely.

🎵 **Sing:** "O Worship the King" (pg 108)

⇁ EXTRA TIME? ⇽
Take a few minutes to write a list of some ways your family participates in ministry at church or in your home. These are spiritual activities that you cannot do on your own - you need God's help! Now discuss how prayer can help you with each of those spiritual activities / ministries.

Mark's Gospel
—— STUDY #5 ——

Seeing Jesus, Not Rules: Part 1/3 "Forgiver"

📖 **Read:** Mark 2:1-12 (Section is 2:1-3:6)

💬 **Talk:**

1. Have you ever been in a crowded room or train? Was it so crowded that no one could sit down? *[answers vary]*

2. What does v2 say about the crowded house? *[there were so many people that they were standing outside the house]*

3. Who came to Jesus in v3? *[four men carrying a paralyzed man]* What does it mean to be paralyzed? *[your back and legs do not work / dependent on everyone else for help]*

4. How did the men get their friend into the house to see Jesus? *[removed part of the roof to let him down]* Jesus saw their faith in God. What did Jesus do? *[forgave his sin]* What a surprise! Jesus' first action proves that our sin problem is more important than any of our physical problems.

5. Some of the religious leaders (the scribes) did not like this. Read v7 again. What part of their thinking was true and what part was false? *[true: only God can forgive sin; false: Jesus wasn't blaspheming because He really IS God]*

6. Which is easier: to SAY you can run fast, or PROVE it by actually running a race? Jesus asks the scribes: "which is easier, to SAY someone's sins are forgiven, or PROVE it by healing the paralyzed man?" (v9)

7. According to v10, why does Jesus heal the man? *[to prove that Jesus has authority to forgive sins]*

8. If the religious leaders saw Jesus as the Messiah instead of only seeing their rules, how would the story change? *[they would have seen the miracle of healing and believed that He is the Son of God]*

9. These verses aren't primarily about 'being a good friend' or about 'determination to reach Jesus.' This passage teaches us Jesus has authority because He is God!

❤️ **Pray:** Heavenly Father, we believe that You have authority on earth to forgive sin and to heal sickness. While we know Jesus had compassion on the sick, You tell us in Your Word how deadly our spiritual sickness is. Jesus serves our most important spiritual need - forgiving our sins, and He also serves our physical needs - one day removing all diseases. Thank You, God!

🎵 **Sing:** Sing "Be Thou My Vision" together as a family. (pg 97)   Also, "His Mercy is More" (not included).

⇉ EXTRA TIME? ⇇

As Mark writes this section, he is telling us how important it is to see Jesus and not just the rules that religion creates. Take your Bible and point out that 1) Mark 2:1-12 proves Jesus has authority to forgive sin. 2) 2:13-22 teach us two lessons through eating and fasting. 3) 2:23-3:6 reveal that Jesus is Lord of the Sabbath day.

Mark's Gospel

STUDY #6

Seeing Jesus, Not Rules: Part 2/3 "Eating"

📖 **Read:** Mark 2:13-22 (Section is 2:1-3:6)

💬 **Talk:**

1. Who did Jesus call to become one of his twelve closest disciples? *[Levi the tax collector]* In v16, the scribes ask, "Why does He eat with sinners?"

2. Why do you think Jesus ate meals and spent time with "sinners"? *[Jesus came to earth to save sinners and show them God's love, Luke 19:10]* Why do you think the scribes and Pharisees didn't spend time with "sinners" or try to help them? *[because they thought themselves better than other people, and didn't want their reputation for 'holiness' to be questioned because of being around "sinners"]*

3. The scribes had rules that forbid them from being friends with sinners or sick people. Jesus spent time with those people and preached the truth to them.

4. Jesus gives the scribes a very clear answer in v17. Do you think Jesus was just talking about healing people's bodies, or also healing their relationship with God? *[spiritual healing too]*

5. The next topic that Mark tells us about involves eating... sort of. What is fasting? *[spiritual discipline where we spend time praying when we would normally be eating; fasting focuses our minds on prayer and devotion to God]*

6. In vs19-20 Jesus uses a word picture to answer the people - what is it? *[the picture of a groom]* The illustration of the bridegroom explains that Jesus will not always be physically present with His disciples. Where did He eventually go? *[to heaven]*

7. In vs21-22 Jesus gives two more illustrations. Both tell us how the kingdom of God is something new that is different from what people expected. What are the two illustrations? *[patching clothing holes and storing new wine in old wineskins (bags)]*

❤️ **Pray:** Father, thank You for loving us even though our sin is ugly. Help us not to be prejudiced or judgmental toward other people, looking down on them because of sin or bad choices, because You forgive us too.

🎵 **Sing:** Philippians 2:5 challenges us to imitate Jesus. Being Jesus' disciple means acting and thinking like Him! Sing "May the Mind of Christ My Savior". (pg 107)

⇒ EXTRA TIME? ⇐

Jesus serves the most unlovely people. This is good news for kids who are bullied or feel like no one loves them. Jesus has power and authority, but he's not a bully. Jesus loves the outcasts and is a friend of people that aren't "cool." No one is beyond Jesus' love. That means that no one is beyond our love too. Is there anyone at school or in your neighborhood that annoys you or that is unlovely? If we serve like Jesus, we will serve them too.

Mark's Gospel

— STUDY #7 —

Seeing Jesus, Not Rules: Part 3/3 "Sabbath"

Read: Mark 2:23-3:6 (Section is 2:1-3:6)

Talk:

1. Have you ever tried to put on clothes too small for you? Think of trying to put on a baby's clothes. How do you think you would look? Could you breathe? *[no! It would be so tight and funny looking!]*
2. In this passage, what were Jesus' disciples doing that the Pharisees didn't like? *[they were picking grain on the Sabbath day]* By the Pharisees' rules, doing hard work on the Sabbath wasn't legal. What was the Sabbath? *[the day God gave to Israel through Moses - a day of rest from physical work so they could do spiritual 'work']*
3. Jesus teaches that the Sabbath was given to help people and teach them something about God. The Sabbath wasn't given to squish people into a rigid system of rules. The Sabbath is designed to serve man (v27). What does Jesus claim to be in v28? *[Lord of the Sabbath]* A day of worship was meant to help people; people weren't created to fit into the sabbath… it is like squeezing into baby's clothes! It just doesn't fit!
4. The next section of verses (3:1-6) tells how Jesus proved His lordship by healing a man's hand right in front of the Pharisees.
5. Why did the Pharisees accuse Jesus of breaking the Sabbath? *[because if Jesus healed the man, then He was doing 'work', and breaking the Sabbath rest]*
6. Jesus asks the Pharisees if the Sabbath is about 1) not working or 2) doing right. Why do you think they didn't answer? *[because they knew they were wrong]* Read v5 - why was Jesus angry and grieved? *[because their hearts were hard]*
7. The passage today teaches us that it is possible to know what God's Word says, but misunderstand it. Who helps us understand what God's Word means and to interpret the Bible? *[Jesus helps us understand. He is the Lord of the Sabbath, and He gets to tell us what is right and wrong]*

Pray: Father, as we read Your Word every day, help us see Jesus and not just rules to obey. We want to obey all Your commands out of love and thankfulness. Thank you for the joy we have to read about Jesus in the pages of scripture. Even when people opposed Him, Jesus followed the will of the Father - we want to follow Your will too.

Sing: Sing "May the Mind of Christ My Savior" (pg 107)

BEING JESUS' DISCIPLE REQUIRES HUMILITY

Mark's Gospel
— STUDY #8 —

Conflict and Desires

📖 **Read:** Mark 3:7-21

💬 **Talk:**

1. When there is conflict between people, it is often because they desire, or want, different things and believe that other people will keep them from getting what they want.

2. Read vs7-8 again. How many times does Mark tell us the size of the crowd? *[two times]* In vs7-12, what did the crowd desire? *[to be close to Jesus and be healed by Him]*

3. In vs13-19, Jesus chooses twelve disciples and their names are listed. In verses 14-15, what are the three jobs Jesus gave His disciples?

   - *[They are to be "with Him" - disciples at that time lived with their teacher and followed the teacher everywhere.*
   - *They will be sent out to preach - in the book of Acts the twelve disciples are also called "apostles", or "sent-out ones".*
   - *They are given authority to cast out demons. As the disciples were sent out to preach and spread the gospel, they followed Jesus' example]*

4. From this section (vs13-19), what did Jesus desire? *[to select disciples to serve closely with Him]* Did the disciples obey that call and follow Jesus? *[yes]*

5. Now read vs20-21. Jesus went back to the town Capernaum. Was His family proud of Him and did they celebrate the coming of God's kingdom? *[no, they thought He was crazy, or "beside himself"]*

6. Do you think Jesus' family members believed His teaching, or did not believe? *[they did not believe]*

7. What did Jesus' family desire? *[They wanted Jesus to stop preaching to big crowds and come home with them]* Did Jesus listen to them and stop, or continue obeying God's will for Him? *[He continued to obey God rather than man]*

❤️ **Pray:** God of heaven, we know that every person in the world desires different things, but we desire to learn Your ways and follow You. Help us to change our desires and cheerfully obey You. Even when other people around us misunderstand Your work, help us love these people but still obey You.

🎵 **Sing:** Sing "I Have Decided to Follow Jesus" and consider how Jesus continued to walk closely with God through His life. (pg 104)

⇶ EXTRA TIME? ⇷

Jesus chose twelve disciples when the needs around Him were very great. Moses needed help in Exodus 18 and did something similar. While this is not the main point of the passage, discuss the wisdom of getting help and not doing ministry all alone. Moses' authority came from God. Jesus' authority came from Himself, because He IS God.

Mark's Gospel
STUDY #9

Choosing Sides

📖 **Read:** Mark 3:22-35

💬 **Talk:**

1. The scribes traveled north from Jerusalem to criticize Jesus. The Pharisees didn't come, they sent their scribes instead. As they watched Jesus preach and heal people, they made an awful accusation about Jesus. In v22, what was the lie? *[that Jesus' power to cast out demons came from Satan]*

2. Sometimes when your friends argue, do they try to get you to "choose sides"? The scribes were accusing Jesus of being on Satan's side and that His power was satanic. What is Jesus' answer in v23? *[why would Satan heal people of demon possession? That doesn't make sense!]* Jesus explained that His authority and power did not come from Satan, because all Jesus' actions are undoing what sin has ruined.

3. Jesus then teaches that in order to rescue people from the slavery of their sin and demon possession, the demons must be cast out (v27).

4. Jesus gave them a strong warning in vs28-29. These verses tell us that attributing to Satan what is accomplished by God reveals that a person is not a believer, a real Christian. It is an awful thing to accuse Jesus of doing Satan's work! Jesus served His heavenly Father for His entire life.

5. Jesus was loyal to God over any desire or relationship He had. Who came to see Jesus in v31? *[Jesus' mother and brothers]* Remember Mark 3:20-21 from the previous study? Jesus' family didn't believe He was the Messiah. The crowd around Jesus thought that He would give special privileges and treatment for His own family, but what does Jesus say in v35? *[people who obey God are His closest relationships]*

6. Being a part of God's family is not something we have by birth. We aren't followers of Jesus just because our parents follow Jesus. We become part of God's family when we follow Jesus by repenting and believing. Note: Jesus' brother James eventually became a Christian and even pastored the church in Jerusalem.

❤️ **Pray:** Father, even if our closest relatives discourage us from following You, we know for certain that choosing to live for You is always the right choice, even when it isn't easy.

🎵 **Sing:** "I Have Decided" gives a firm picture of what it means to choose to follow God. (pg 104)

⇋ EXTRA TIME? ⇋

Read Matthew 10:37-39 and answer this question: If Jesus made His relationship with God more important than any other relationship on earth, was it then right for Him to ask the same thing of His disciples?

Mark's Gospel
STUDY #10

Jesus' Teaching: 1/3 "Hidden in Plain Sight"

Read: Mark 4:1-12 (Section 4:1-34)

Talk:

1. Imagine you are going on a vacation. Your parents will not tell you where you are going, but they still talk about the trip in front of you. They don't want to give you any clues, so they use words that make sense to them, but not you. Would you like to be left out like that? Would you really, really, really love to know what they're talking about? *[allow answers]*

2. In the passage today, Jesus begins to teach in parables to the crowds that follow Him. Parables are stories that teach a lesson. People with stubborn, hard hearts did not understand the parables very well and did not want to. Tender-hearted, trusting people asked God to help them understand what parables meant.

3. What were the 4 types of soil in Jesus' parable of the sower? *[along the path, rocky ground, thorny soil, and good soil]* In the next study we will talk about what Jesus was teaching with this parable.

4. But for now, read v12 again. This section in Mark (4:1-34) tells us what people were **hearing** from Jesus. The next section after this (4:35-6:6) tells us what people **saw** Jesus do. Each gospel writer chose to tell people only a little bit of what Jesus did and said. Mark's outline for the next few chapters reveals what people **heard** and **saw** Jesus do, following the quote in 4:12. Some people responded with faith, most did not.

5. Let's talk about spiritual pride. What do you think spiritual pride is? *[allow answers]* Everyone struggles with pride. A spiritually proud person thinks he is better than other people because of all the religious things he or she does.

6. Spiritual pride also makes you spiritually blind. The scribes and Pharisees didn't want to understand Jesus' teaching. They didn't want to hear the truth. But who *did* want to hear Jesus (v10)? *[the disciples]* How about you?

Pray: Heavenly Father, thank You for sending Your Son Jesus to teach us Who You are and what You are like. We are very proud, but want to humbly learn from Jesus. Open our ears to hear the truth from the Bible. Open our eyes to see wonderful things out of Your Word.

Sing: Sing "Be Thou My Vision" as your family reflects on the devotional for today. (pg 97) Also, "Behold Our God" (not included in hymn section).

⇒ EXTRA TIME? ⇐
Look over the verses for today again. Can you find the sentence where Jesus is encouraging people to hear? Remember, hearing means more than understanding Jesus' words. Hearing means being a humble student of God. It will look like "who has ears to hear let him hear." Did you find which verse it's found in?

Mark's Gospel
— STUDY #11 —
Jesus' Teaching: 2/3 "Listen Carefully"

📖 **Read:** Mark 4:13-25 (Section 4:1-34)

💬 **Talk:**

1. To review, read Mark 4:12. This section on "Jesus' Teaching" tells us what people were **hearing** from Jesus. Mark's outline for the next few chapters reveals what people **heard** and **saw** Jesus do, in that order. Some people responded with faith, most did not.

2. In the parable of the sower, Jesus teaches that God's Word is like seed spread all over the ground. There are four 'soils' in this parable:

3. *V15- The path* - this person's heart is unwilling to hear the truth. Satan steals the seed away. Some people reject God's Word the moment they hear.

4. *V.16- The rocky ground* - this person likes to hear the good parts of God's Word, but never wants to sacrifice anything for God. Once they realize that following Jesus costs something, they give up.

5. *V18- The thorny soil* - this person's heart is like a plant that grows too close to weeds. God's truth looks like it may be changing the person, but no real or lasting fruit ever grows on the plant. This person becomes distracted by possessions and other things, losing focus on God.

6. *V20- The good soil* - this person allows God's Word to change them and make them more like Jesus in their words and actions and attitudes. This change is called "fruit."

7. If you are a Christian, what "fruit" has God's Word been growing in your life? *[allow answers]*

8. In vs21-25, Jesus teaches that the kingdom of God brings light into a dark world. Whenever Jesus taught, people's attitudes toward God were revealed. Think about the last several devotionals: sin, hard hearts, and true believers are all easier to understand because of Jesus' teaching.

❤️ **Pray:** Father, anything good that comes out of our hearts is because of Your Word which changes us from the inside out. As we study Your Word, we are willing to hear it, believe it, and be changed by it. Whatever fruit You choose to grow in our lives, we want it to honor You and help other people to see You more clearly because of it. Thank You!

🎵 **Sing:** "This Is My Father's World" Keep in mind the parable of the sower. God makes His creation grow and He also helps us grow spiritually. (pg 110)

⇉ EXTRA TIME? ⇇
Search the verses for today. Can you find the sentence where Jesus is encouraging people to hear? Remember, hearing means more than understanding Jesus' words. Hearing means being a humble student of God.

Mark's Gospel
STUDY #12

Jesus' Teaching: 3/3 "Meager to Mighty"

📖 **Read:** Mark 4:26-34 (Section 4:1-34)

💬 **Talk:**

1. Remember Mark 4:12. This section of Mark tells us what people were **hearing** from Jesus.

2. Kaboom! If the entrance of God's kingdom on earth was to make a sound, that's what the Jewish leaders expected when the Kingdom arrived. They expected big noises, flashing holy light, shining armor, a mighty Messiah who leads God's chosen people into a new and lasting era of triumph on the earth - a mighty kingdom that arrives suddenly! Kaboom!

3. But is that what happened? Jesus the Messiah arrived on earth in a stable. He grew up in a poor town of unimportant people. Jesus didn't have His own home as He traveled and taught. Even when Jesus died, He was buried in a borrowed tomb. So, did Jesus look anything like the Messiah the Jews expected to see? *[No!]*

4. The two parables in today's passage are about seeds, and they teach the same lesson about God's kingdom. The kingdom's arrival was NOT big and was NOT sudden when it started. Have you ever waited for a garden to grow? *[allow answers - gardens grow slowly and take a lot of work to get started, but when the time is right there is fruit to pick and eat!]*

5. Even if it is hard to see, God's kingdom keeps growing. God knows exactly when is the right time for His Kingdom to be fully ready. When Jesus returns to earth, it will be the right time. Little bit by little bit, God's Kingdom is growing from meager to mighty. God IS working in the world, even when it is hard to see.

6. You can trust God that He is growing His kingdom, even if it's hard to notice.

❤️ **Pray:** God, maybe someday soon Your kingdom will be fully grown and ready to go! Your Son *will* return and the kingdom *will* finally look like the mighty Messiah who leads Your people into a new and lasting era of triumph on the earth! However humbly and unnoticeably Your kingdom grows, it has been growing and growing to this very day! Thank You for making us a part of Your work in this world.

🎵 **Sing:** Sing "Jesus Shall Reign" to remember how Jesus came to earth humbly, but will return one day in power. (pg 106)   Also, "Come Behold the Wondrous Mystery" (not included in hymn section).

⇉ EXTRA TIME? ⇇

Remember that Mark 4 explains the importance of really hearing the truth. Hearing means more than understanding Jesus' words. Hearing means being a humble student of God. The next section in Mark explains what people saw Jesus do.

Mark's Gospel
STUDY #13

Seeing Jesus: 1/4 "Power Over Creation"

📖 **Read:** Mark 4:35-41 (Section 4:35-5:43)

💬 **Talk:** *Four truths - Seeing Jesus' Power and Authority*

1. Jesus sent the disciples into the storm *on purpose*. (vs35-37)
   - Do you think the storm was a surprise to Jesus? *[no]* Was it a surprise to the disciples? *[maybe, the Bible doesn't tell us for sure]*
   - When you face storms in life, like fearful things that you didn't know would happen, do you think they surprise Jesus, too? *[no]*
   - Our trials in life are not random; God allows them for His good purposes.

2. Jesus' mighty power is *cause for calm*. (v38) The disciples were so panicked and scared that they question Christ's love for them. They accused Jesus of no longer caring for them.
   - Have you ever felt that way when you were afraid or suffering?
   - Jesus was asleep in the boat. This tells us two things: 1) Jesus was physically tired after the day of preaching and teaching. 2) Jesus wasn't afraid of the storm.
   - Fear is normal because people don't have power over storms. In our fearful response we, like the disciples, accuse God of not caring about the storm or the fear. Did Jesus care? *[yes]*

3. Jesus controlled the storm *instantly*. (v39-40)
   - We know Jesus cared because He stopped the storm immediately. What kind of calm was there after the storm? *[great/completely/perfectly calm]*

4. Don't hurry to be done today - notice this! The disciples feared greatly *after the storm*. (v41) Why? They recognized the presence of the One they were with! Is there any difference in the fear they had of the storm and the fear they had of Jesus' power? *[answers will vary, guide the children to understand types of fear]*

❤️ **Pray:** Father, thank You for showing us Your power in the pages of scripture! We praise You for Your authority and Your power over creation. We thank you for Your unfailing love. Storms, wind, and floods are all very powerful, but none of them is more powerful than Jesus' words. When we think of what Jesus is able to do, we fear You in awe and love You all the more!

🎵 **Sing:** "God Moves in a Mysterious Way" (pg 103)

⇉ EXTRA TIME? ⇇

Read Psalm 107:23-31 together, then talk about trials that God has brought you or your family through. Focus on God's unfailing love more than the suffering or despair. The goal is to discuss with your children how God works, and how trials help us see Jesus more clearly.

Mark's Gospel
STUDY #14

Seeing Jesus: 2/4 "Power Over Demons"

📖 **Read:** Mark 5:1-20 (Section 4:35-5:43)

💬 **Talk:**

1. In this section of the Gospel of Mark, the people and disciples following Jesus saw Him fulfill Isaiah 6:9-10. They saw Jesus do mighty works and miracles - some understood Who Jesus is, some did not.

2. In today's passage, Jesus and the disciples have crossed the Sea of Galilee to a Gentile region. Do you know who "Gentile" refers to? *[anyone who is not Jewish]* This region to the east of Galilee is Decapolis, a land where mostly Gentiles lived.

3. In your own words, describe what happens in this account. *[younger children may need help recalling the events step-by-step]* If you have enough people available, consider having family members act out the story while a child or parent narrates.

4. When Jesus asked the demon to give its name, what was the answer? *[Legion, meaning 'many']* Around two thousand pigs were driven off the cliff by the demons that Jesus cast out, so it is possible there were that many demons possessing that man! Read vs3-4 again and you can understand how powerful the demons were.

5. Did all the demons obey Jesus? *[yes]* Why? *[because Jesus is God, the Creator of everything]*

6. The healed man wanted to follow Jesus, but Jesus said no. Read vs19-20 and explain why. *[Jesus did not allow the man to become one His close disciples because Jesus wanted the man to tell others about Him]*

7. How are the instructions Jesus gave in Mark 1:44 different than the instructions He gave in Mark 5:43? *[Jesus wanted the healed man to share the good news, not keep it a secret]*

8. Compare Mark 5:17 with 7:32. The first time Jesus visited Decapolis, they begged Him to do what? *[leave]* Then the next time He came, the crowd begged Jesus to heal people. Do you think the demon-possessed man obeyed Jesus and told others about Him? *[yes, lots of people knew Who Jesus was by the time He returned to Decapolis later on]*

❤️ **Pray:** God in heaven, You have created everything in the universe. You created the things we can see and touch, and the spiritual things we can't see, like angels. We confess that Jesus is God, and that He has power over creation and demons. Thank you for showing us both Your power and Your mercy.

🎵 **Sing:** "I Sing the Mighty Power of God" (pg 105)

→ **BEING JESUS' DISCIPLE MEANS OBEYING GOD** ←

Mark's Gospel
— STUDY #15 —

Seeing Jesus: 3/4 "Power Over Sickness"

📖 **Read:** Mark 5:21-34 (Section 4:35-5:43)

💬 **Talk:**

1. What was the name of the religious ruler who came to Jesus? *[Jairus]* What did he beg Jesus to do? *[heal his daughter before she died]*

2. As a Pharisee in charge of the local synagogue, it is surprising that Jairus fell at Jesus' feet and begged for help. What does this tell you about Jairus? *[he sincerely needed Jesus' help and humbly admitted it]*

3. "Rock, paper, scissors" is a familiar game with familiar principles: scissors wins over paper, but loses to rock, etc. When it comes to the Jewish ceremonial cleanness, the bad *always* wins over the good, that is to say, to be ceremonially clean you must *completely avoid what is unclean*. To touch something or someone unclean was to automatically become unclean yourself! No questions asked! (Numbers 5:1-4)

4. A woman sick for many years reached out to Jesus for healing. Her illness made her 'unclean' and yucky. Have you ever felt that way? Gross or dirty? Anyone who made direct contact with her would be considered unclean for a time. Jesus, however, did not avoid her (as the religious leaders of the day might). Jesus allowed contact with the untouchable, and it sent clear messages in that day. The Pharisees wouldn't have gotten near her. But Jesus did.

5. Her healing shows the power and holiness of the Savior: that contact with Him, in faith, *makes unclean things clean.* The woman who couldn't attend the temple for twelve years, now could. She couldn't hug her family members without making them unclean for Jewish ceremonies, but after Jesus healed her now she could wrap her arms around them. Similar to "Rock, Paper, Scissors", Jesus' power and holiness 'wins' over sin, the curse, and death. Every time.

❤️ **Pray:** What a wonderful Savior is Jesus our Lord! Father, thank You for proving both Your power over sickness and Your love for people. Sometimes we feel that our problems are too great, or have lasted too long for anything to ever change. But we see today that Jesus' love and power can change things in an instant.

🎵 **Sing:** "Come My Soul with Every Care". While the religious leaders treated sick people coldly, Jesus warmly loved and cared for them. (pg 100)   Also, "Wonderful, Merciful Savior" (not included in hymn section).

⇉ EXTRA TIME? ⇇
Take out any Legos, figurines, or paper dolls you may have in your home, and recreate a picture of what this story might have looked like. Ask the children to describe how the following characters would have acted if the woman had come to them for help instead of coming to Jesus: the Pharisees, Jairus, the disciples, or the crowd.

Mark's Gospel
STUDY #16

Seeing Jesus: 4/4 "Power Over Death"

Read: Mark 5:35-43 (Section 4:35-5:43)

Talk:

1. So far in this section we have seen Jesus revealing His power and authority to the people around Him. We have seen His power over creation, and demons, and sickness. Now we see that Jesus even has power over death.

2. You may remember from the last study that Jesus was on His way to Jairus' house when He stopped to heal a woman. We read today that Jesus was "too late" to heal the girl before she died.

3. When Jesus arrived at the house, what did He tell the people there? *[that the girl was only sleeping]* How did the people respond? *[they laughed at Him]*

4. Before we think of those people as awful and faithless, put yourself in their times. Was death final in their mind? *[yes]* Did anyone ever come back after dying? *[no]* Did they believe in a resurrection? *[some did, but little was known about it]* From their viewpoint, what Jesus said was crazy and maybe insensitive. But Jesus wasn't just a man, Jesus was God.

5. From a human's perspective, was the situation hopeless? Was it too late? *[yes]* From God's perspective, was the situation hopeless? Was it too late? *[not at all]*

6. Do you think Jairus' faith in God was stronger because Jesus was delayed from reaching the house? Think of it: Do you think Jairus believed in God's power more because Jesus didn't just heal a sick girl, He raised a dead girl back to life? *[yes]*

7. How do you respond when God doesn't answer your requests right away? *[allow answers]* God waits until the right time to reveal His will and make Himself more clearly seen. You can trust Him and wait patiently for Him!

Pray: Father, You know all things. You know the best time to act. You know the best way to answer our requests. You are God, and we are not. So we trust You to glorify Yourself and make Your mighty name known. What a mighty God You are, that even death was not final for Jesus at the cross, nor will death be final for Christians. We look forward to the day when we will be with You in Your kingdom!

Sing: "Christ the Lord is Risen Today" (pg 98)

⇒ BEING JESUS' DISCIPLE MEANS HOPING IN GOD'S POWER ⇐

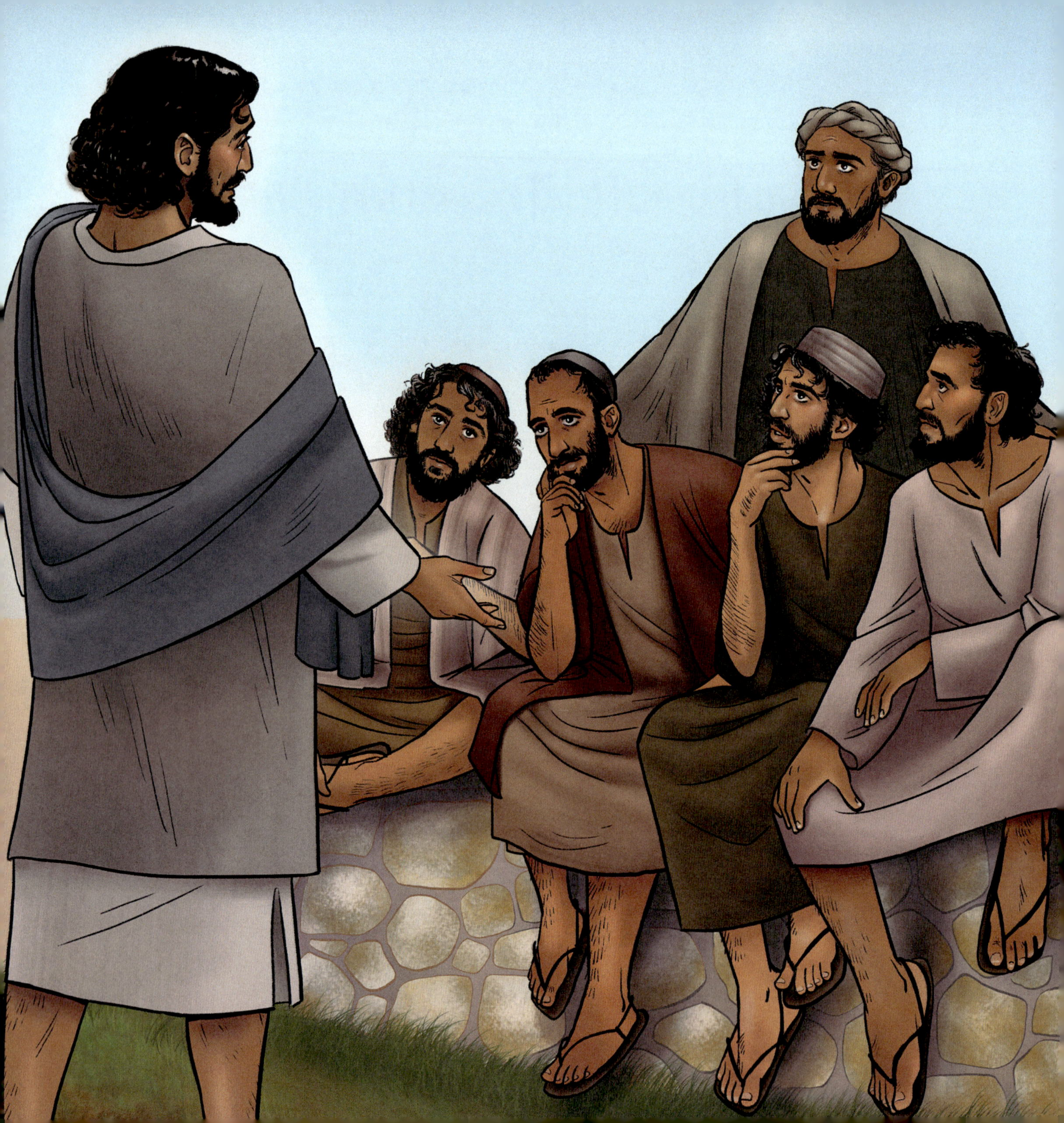

Mark's Gospel
STUDY #17

Commitment to Jesus

📖 **Read:** Mark 6:7-30

💬 **Talk:**

1. Go back and read Mark 3:14-15. Jesus' plan for His disciples included sharing in the preaching and healing ministry.

2. In vs8-9, the disciples were to "travel light", meaning they were not to pack bags and extra clothes, but get right to the task of preaching repentance and the coming kingdom of God. Why do you think Jesus sent them out in groups of two? *[answers vary, but ministry is seldom meant to be accomplished alone]*

3. In that time, the Pharisees taught the Jewish people to symbolically shake the dust off their feet when leaving Gentile lands and entering Jewish territory. When the disciples' message was rejected in a town, why were they to shake the dust off their feet? *[because the people there had rejected God and would answer to God for that rebellious decision; the disciples had done their part by preaching]*

4. Have you ever seen dark rain clouds in the distant horizon that cast dark shadows on the earth? What do those clouds mean for the near future? *[a storm is on the way]*

5. Vs21-30 cast a dark shadow on the future for Jesus' ministry. If John the Baptist was killed for preaching the truth, the question we ask ourselves as we read is, "What, then, will happen to Jesus?"

6. Did Herod really want to have John killed? (v26) *[no, but his reputation and power would look weak if he didn't honor his boastful promise to the girl]*

7. Was John the Baptist a failure because he was killed by Herod? *[no, he lived to honor God and obeyed God in his life]*

8. John the Baptist lived to "shine a spotlight" on Jesus, and once Jesus started His ministry, John allowed himself to become less important, known, and listened to. What lesson can we learn from John's example? *[that we should live to let Jesus be more clearly seen and loved, not ourselves]*

❤️ **Pray:** God, wherever You send us in life, we want to spread the good news about Jesus. All people on earth must hear about Jesus and the gospel, so we will tell the people we know about You.

🎵 **Sing:** Sing "I Have Decided to Follow Jesus" today. (pg 104)

⇉ EXTRA TIME? ⇇
Take a moment to connect this study with the idea of service - that following Jesus is about serving Jesus by making him look great, even when it costs us. In your culture and in your country, what are the costs for following Jesus and being His disciple?

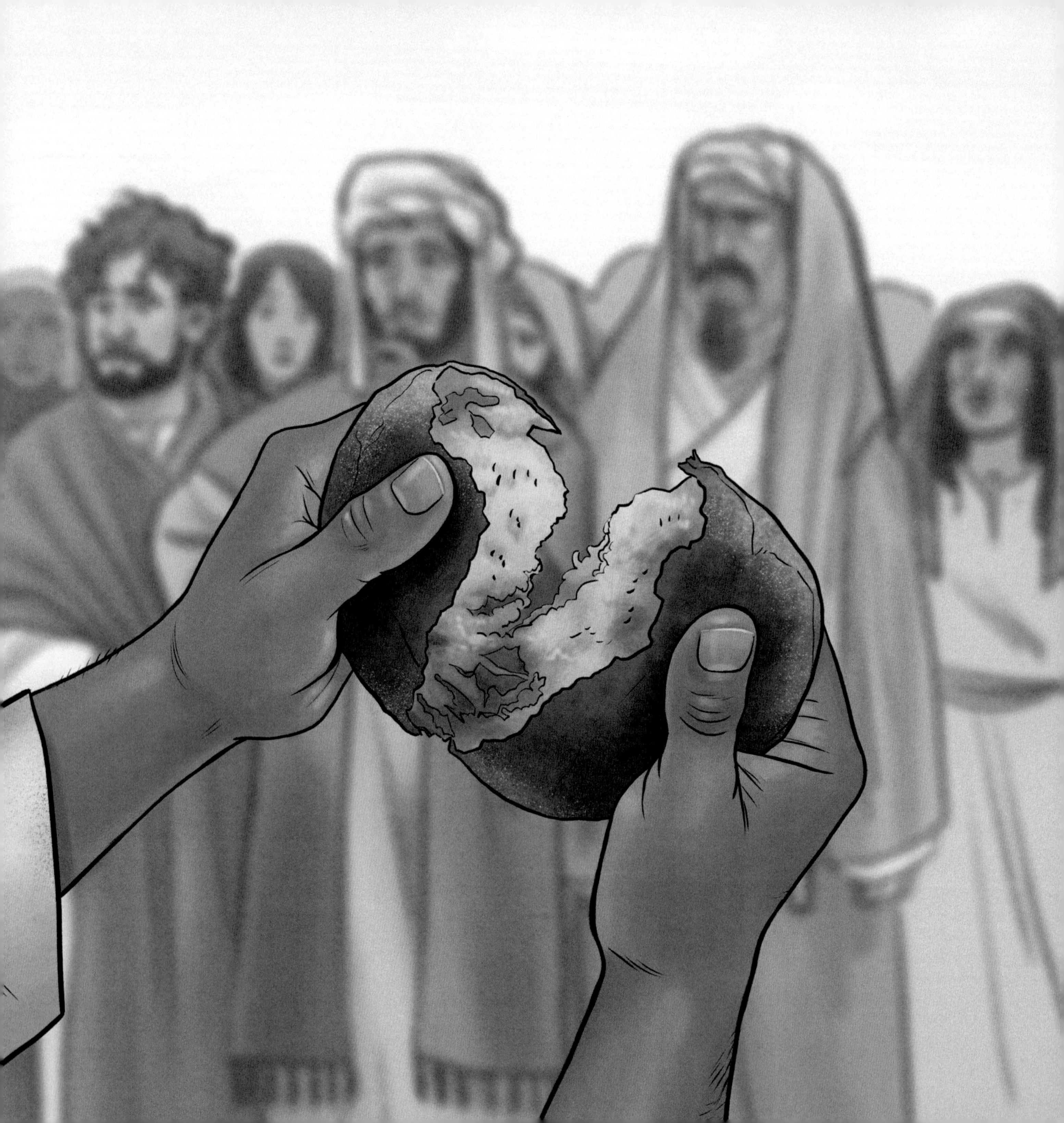

Mark's Gospel
STUDY #18
Bread & Water

📖 **Read:** Mark 6:30-52

💬 **Talk:**

*** While "The Feeding of the 5,000" and "Jesus Walking on Water" are well-known accounts, review both stories so the children understand what was read today. ***

1. In this study we want to notice a few little things. Did anyone notice the first word of v45? It's an action word! (see "Extra Time?" From Study #3) Jesus and the disciples spent much of the day preaching and feeding over 5,000 people. *Immediately* after that, Jesus sent the disciples across the Sea of Galilee.

2. What did Jesus do after He sent the disciples away? *[dismiss crowd and spend time in prayer]* Do you think it is just as important to pray *after* a big day of ministry as it is to pray *before* a big day of ministry? *[yes, it seems so!]*

3. At the end of v48, did you notice what it looked like Jesus was going to do? *[He looked as though He would walk right past them heading to the other side]*

4. Read vs51-52. Mark says that the disciples were shocked at Jesus walking on water because they did not understand about the loaves. Why? (v52) *[because their hearts were hard; they misunderstood the lesson of the bread]*

- Why would Jesus walking on water have anything to do with Jesus feeding the crowds earlier in the day? *[let the children attempt to answer]*

- When Jesus fed the 5,000 earlier that day the disciples should have understood that Jesus was God and grown confident in that fact. But they didn't understand that truth, so when Jesus came walking on the water, they were shocked. Had they realized Jesus is God and can do anything, the struggle of faith and fear would not have been so difficult for them.

❤️ **Pray:** Heavenly Father, You have told us many things about Yourself in the Bible - You know all things, You see all things, You have all power and hold the universe together. When we pray to You, help us ask in faith according to Your will. Let us see Your answers, so that our faith can be strengthened.

🎵 **Sing:** Sing "Be Thou My Vision" Remember how easily people misunderstood Jesus' reason for coming to earth. Seek God on His terms, not your own. (pg 97)   Also, "Jesus, Thank You" (not included in hymn section).

⇥ EXTRA TIME? ⇤

When Israel was traveling through the wilderness, what did God provide for them to eat? *[manna]* When Israel was stuck between the Red Sea and Pharaoh's army, how did God deliver them? *[walking through the sea]* As Mark placed these "Bread & Water" accounts together, he is asking us to remember how God delivered Israel and how Jesus fed and delivered His followers.

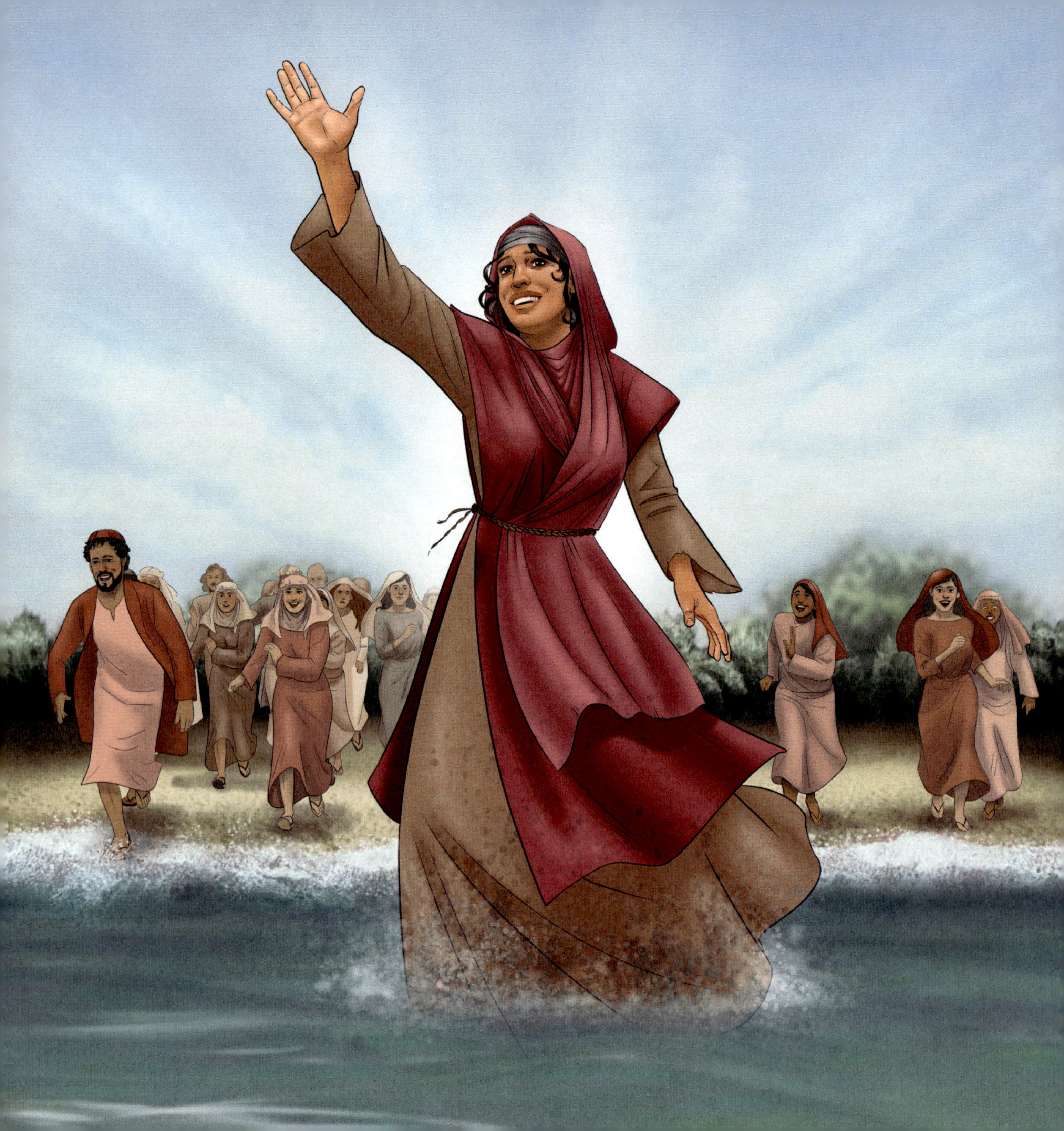

Mark's Gospel
STUDY #19

Unwelcome at Home

📖 **Read:** Mark 6:53-56 and 6:1-6

💬 **Talk:**

1. In the passages today we notice a clear contrast. What are you doing when you contrast two things? *[compare the differences between two things]* While dogs and cats are both pets, there are a lot of ways you can contrast them.

2. Mark starts and ends chapter six with contrasting stories. Both stories involve Jesus and the way other people react to Him. In both Nazareth and Gennesaret, Jesus is immediately recognized. But the two towns respond *very differently*.

3. In Nazareth, how did the people in Jesus' hometown react to Him? (v3) *[they were offended by Him, how popular He had become; they thought Jesus was a poor 'nobody' like any of them]*

    - How did things go while Jesus was there? *[their unbelief made Jesus' healing and preaching ministry more difficult]*

4. In Gennesaret, how did the people react to Him? (vs54-56) *[they immediately recognized Jesus and excitedly "ran about the whole region" spreading the news]*

    - How did things go while Jesus was there? *[they brought all the sick people to public places like markets and streets so that the ill could reach out and touch Jesus' clothes as He walked by. They were excited!]*

5. In this contrast of two villages, we see that Jesus will not force His healing or preaching ministry on anyone. However, willing hearts that are hungry for the truth will be satisfied by Jesus.

6. When you think about your own heart and your attitude toward God, which side of the contrast looks most like you? Are you excited about the things of God? Or do you act like you do not need God or His help?

❤️ **Pray:** You are God and You are holy. Your Word will stand forever, and the opinions of people cannot change Who You are. In all Your unchanging ways, we ask that You continue to change our hearts. When the Bible is taught, read, or preached to us, help us to listen carefully and with open hearts.

🎵 **Sing:** Sing "Amazing Grace" and humbly consider God's grace toward you! (pg 96)

⇒ EXTRA TIME? ⇐

Read Acts 2:41 and then simply ask, "What do you think it looks like when a person 'gladly receives' the Word of God?" Answers will vary, but as you try to look at the question from different angles, be sure to keep the discussion Biblical.

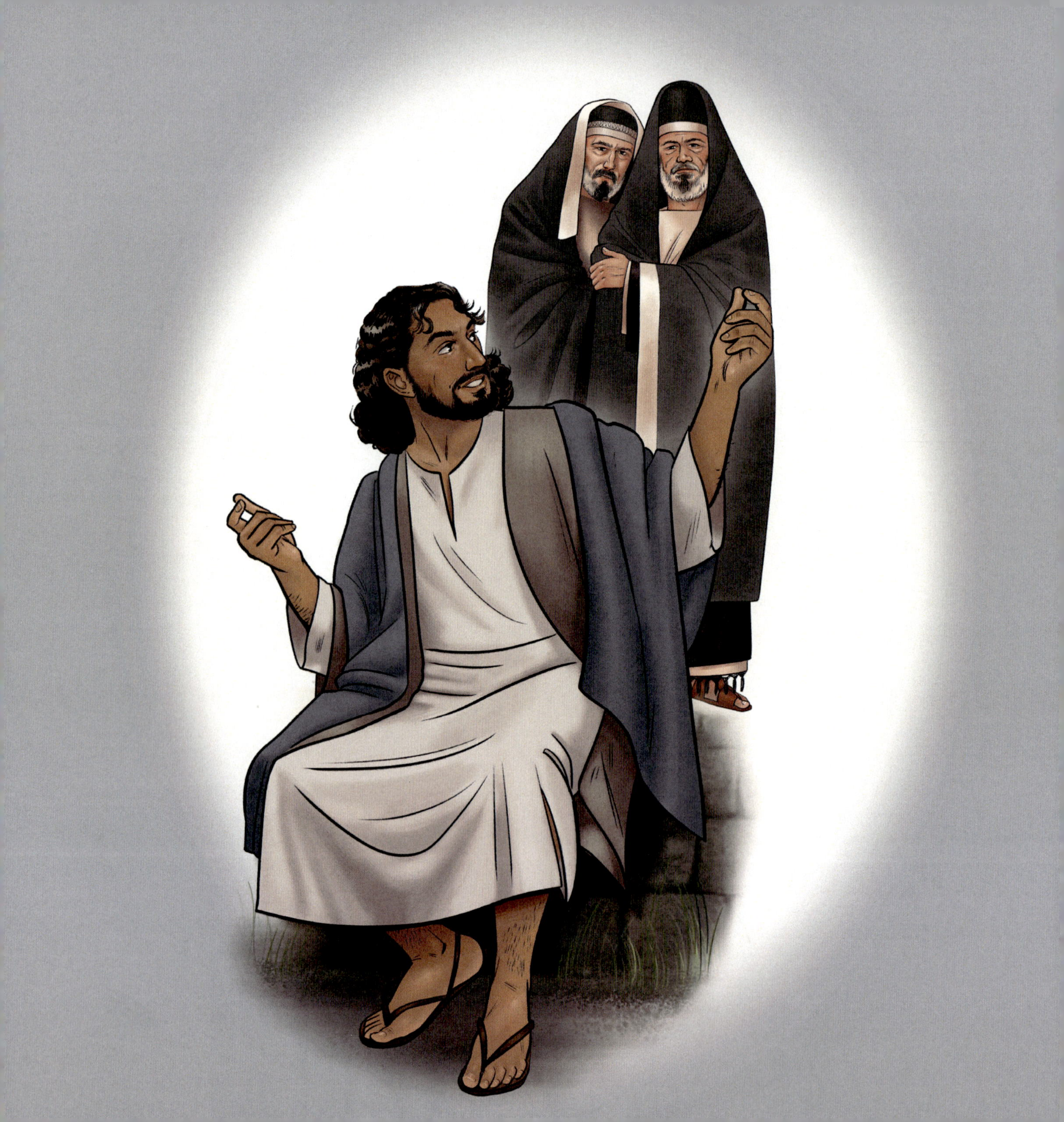

Mark's Gospel
STUDY #20

Wash Up for Supper

📖 **Read:** Mark 7:1-23

💬 **Talk:** "Say 'thank you' to grandma for the cookies."

1. Have you ever seen a child encouraged or even threatened to show gratitude to someone else? Every time someone does something kind for you, it is right to thank them. Yet many children, especially young ones, stubbornly refuse to show gratitude. They mumble, "Fine... thanks" and walk away. Do you think an attitude like that *really* shows gratitude for the cookies that grandma made? *[no!]*

2. While you can force a child to say 'thank you', a parent cannot make it come from the child's heart in genuine thankfulness. Read what Jesus says in v6.

3. Do you think the Pharisees were worshipping God from a genuine heart? *[no]* Jesus points out in this passage that while people can clean up on the outside of their physical body, that God is looking at a person's heart - the spiritual heart.

4. In vs9-13, Jesus gives one example out of many He could have chosen (v13). Have you heard the command, "Honor your father and mother"? Part of Jewish family life involved caring for one's parents in old age. This would take a lot of money and effort to do. The Pharisees allowed people to declare "Corban" and dedicate the money to the temple / God. By doing this, who didn't have enough money to live on? *[elderly parents]* Who did get the money? *[temple, priests and Pharisees]*

5. In vs18-23, Jesus explains that eating dirty food doesn't make a person *spiritually* dirty. This study reveals our greatest problem (our hearts) and our greatest need (forgiveness of sin). Jesus serves us by giving His life as a ransom for our sin problem. The pride, selfishness, and evil that comes out of people's hearts is what "defiles" a person in God's eyes. Jesus teaches that theft, slander, coveting, and pride are a *sin problem*. Failing to wash up for supper is not.

❤️ **Pray:** Father, while man looks on the outward appearance, we know You care about what is coming out of our hearts. When we sin with our words, actions, or thoughts, these are the things that break Your law. Help us keep Your Word in truth, and obey You from genuine hearts of gratitude. No one is forcing us to praise You today, we do it willingly. Help us honor You from our hearts, not just our lips.

🎵 **Sing:** Sing the first couple of verses of "Amazing Grace" out of a thankful, genuine heart. (pg 96)

⇉ BEING JESUS' DISCIPLE MEANS CONFESSING SIN ⇇
Confessing sin means agreeing with God about His laws that you break. If we confess, He forgives.

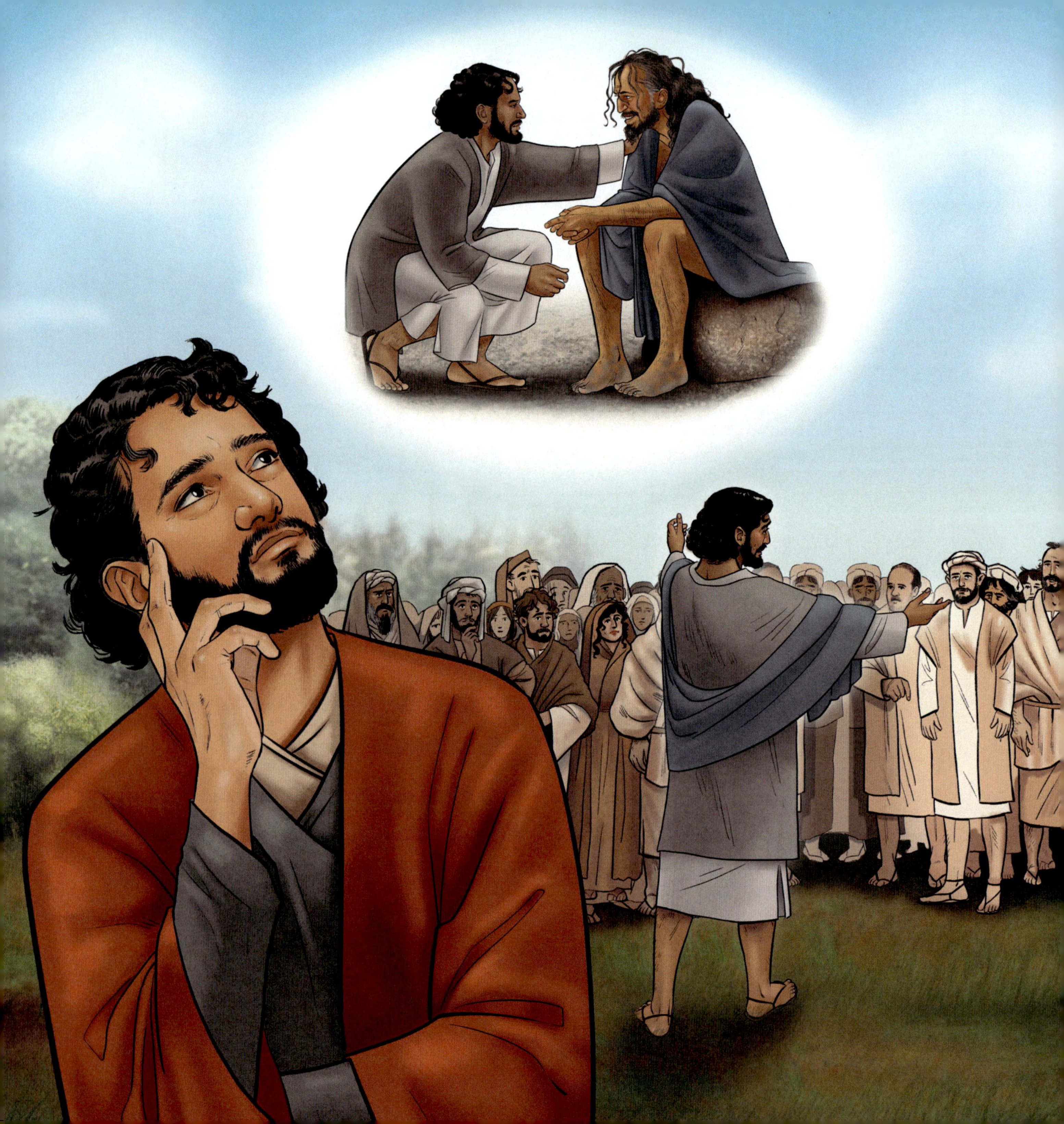

Mark's Gospel
— STUDY #21 —

Jesus Preaches to Gentiles

📖 **Read:** Mark 7:24-37

💬 **Talk:**

1. Jesus preaches in the cities of Tyre and Sidon - vs24-30
   - Tyre and Sidon were cities north of Galilee, over by the Mediterranean Sea.
   - A Gentile woman, meaning a non-Jewish person, came looking for Jesus. What was her daughter's problem? *[unclean spirit / demon possessed]*
   - What do you think about Jesus' response to the woman's request? (v27) *[answers will vary]* Does it seem like Jesus is being rude because she isn't Jewish? *[allow answers]*
   - Jesus was never proud or cruel to people, so we must read this passage carefully. Because of the woman's response in v28, we understand that Jesus was testing just how persistent the woman would be in seeking God's help. Her humble answer reveals that she was desperate for help, yet humble when God answered.
   - Throughout the Bible other Gentiles were not so humble, as with Naaman bathing in the Jordan river. (2 Kings 5)

2. Jesus visits Decapolis again - Vs31-37
   - Remember Study 14, where a demon possessed man could not be contained, but Jesus set him free? Now Jesus returns. Do the people try to send Him away this time? *[no, they welcome Him excitedly]*
   - Now that the Gentiles in Decapolis have heard of Jesus from the healed man, they are willing to hear Him preach.
   - Is it important, then, that the man Jesus healed back in Study #14 stayed in his home area and told others about Jesus? *[yes]* Has Jesus commanded you and me to tell others about Him while we remain on earth? *[yes!]*

❤️ **Pray:** God in heaven, You sent Jesus to be the Savior of the world. Anyone from any nationality or country is important to You. You have made us in Your image and given us life. We will, with Your help, honor You while we live on earth - speaking Your Word and living as Your children. Thank You for rescuing us. We will obey Your Word.

🎵 **Sing:** Sing "May the Mind of Christ My Savior" together in response to the study today. (pg 107)

⇉ **BEING JESUS' DISCIPLE MEANS SPREADING GOOD NEWS** ⇇
Jesus preached the good news of salvation to everyone. He commands us to share the gospel too.

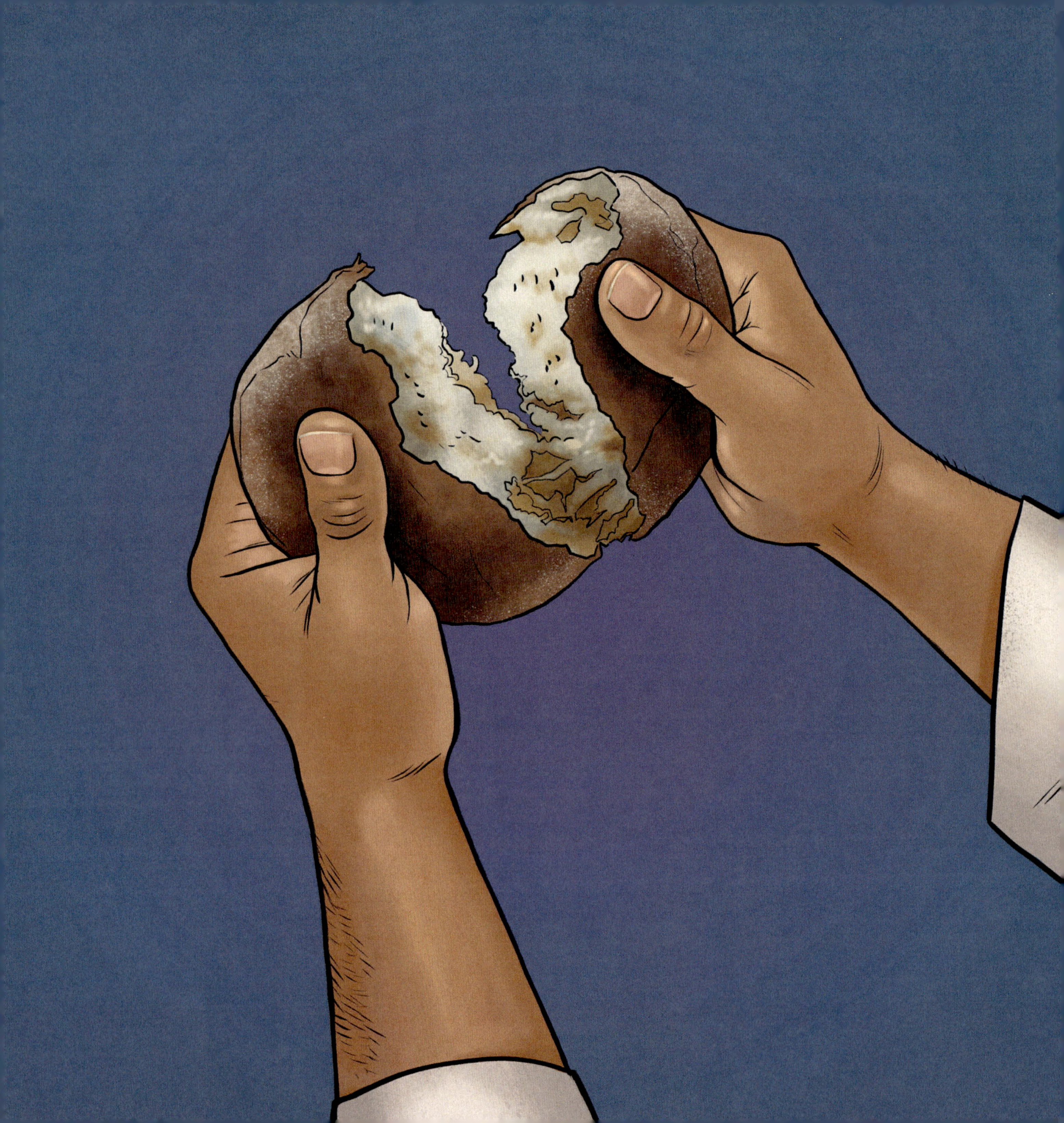

Mark's Gospel
STUDY #22

Second Helpings

📖 **Read:** Mark 8:1-9

💬 **Talk:**

1. Jesus fed 5,000 Jewish people in Study #18; in this section of Mark Jesus feeds a crowd again but it is a Gentile crowd, not Jewish. Mark 8 talks a lot about bread. Is Jesus the Living Bread for both Jews and Gentiles? *[yes]*

2. How many days had the people been with Jesus? *[three days]* Even for people who brought food, do you think they would run out after three days? *[yes]*

3. Have you ever been in a desolate place? Maybe a desert? Can you imagine being hungry and thirsty with no restaurant within hours of walking?

4. Jesus miraculously feeds the entire crowd of 4,000 people. What was the first "course"? (v5) *[bread]* What was the second "course"? (v7) *[dried fish]*

5. We have talked about contrast before in previous studies. Contrast the following observations from these verses:
   - Note how little food was at the start of this meal and how much was at the end.
   - The disciples saw Jesus feed a crowd before, yet seem confused at how they will be fed this time.
   - The people were faint with hunger, but when Jesus left, they were full.

6. Have you ever eaten so much that you could not take another bite? *[likely, yes]* Jesus fills us spiritually like the people were filled physically.

7. As the Bread of Life (John 6:35), Jesus spiritually satisfies our souls like food satisfies our hunger. Notice this: even when our souls are satisfied by Jesus, He offers us even more of Himself.
   - The word for the seven "baskets" in the original language means something more like "big basket", similar to Acts 9 when Paul was lowered down a wall in a *huge* basket. There were seven *huge* baskets of scraps. Jesus satisfies our souls' hunger and there's plenty more after that!
   - In a very real and spiritual sense, we need Jesus to stay alive and healthy just like our bodies need food to stay alive and healthy. When your soul is hungry, turn to Jesus, the Bread of Life!

❤️ **Pray:** Father, we know that nothing satisfies like You do. Possessions wear out and break down. People and relationships will disappoint us, or worse, hurt us. That is why we hope in You, because we would rather have You than to gain the whole world. Thank You for Your great love and care for us!

🎵 **Sing:** "This Is My Father's World" - Nothing in this world was made to replace God in our hearts. Only God satisfies. (pg 110)   Also, "All I Have is Christ" (not included in hymn section).

⇒ **BEING JESUS' DISCIPLE MEANS HUNGERING FOR GOD** ⇐

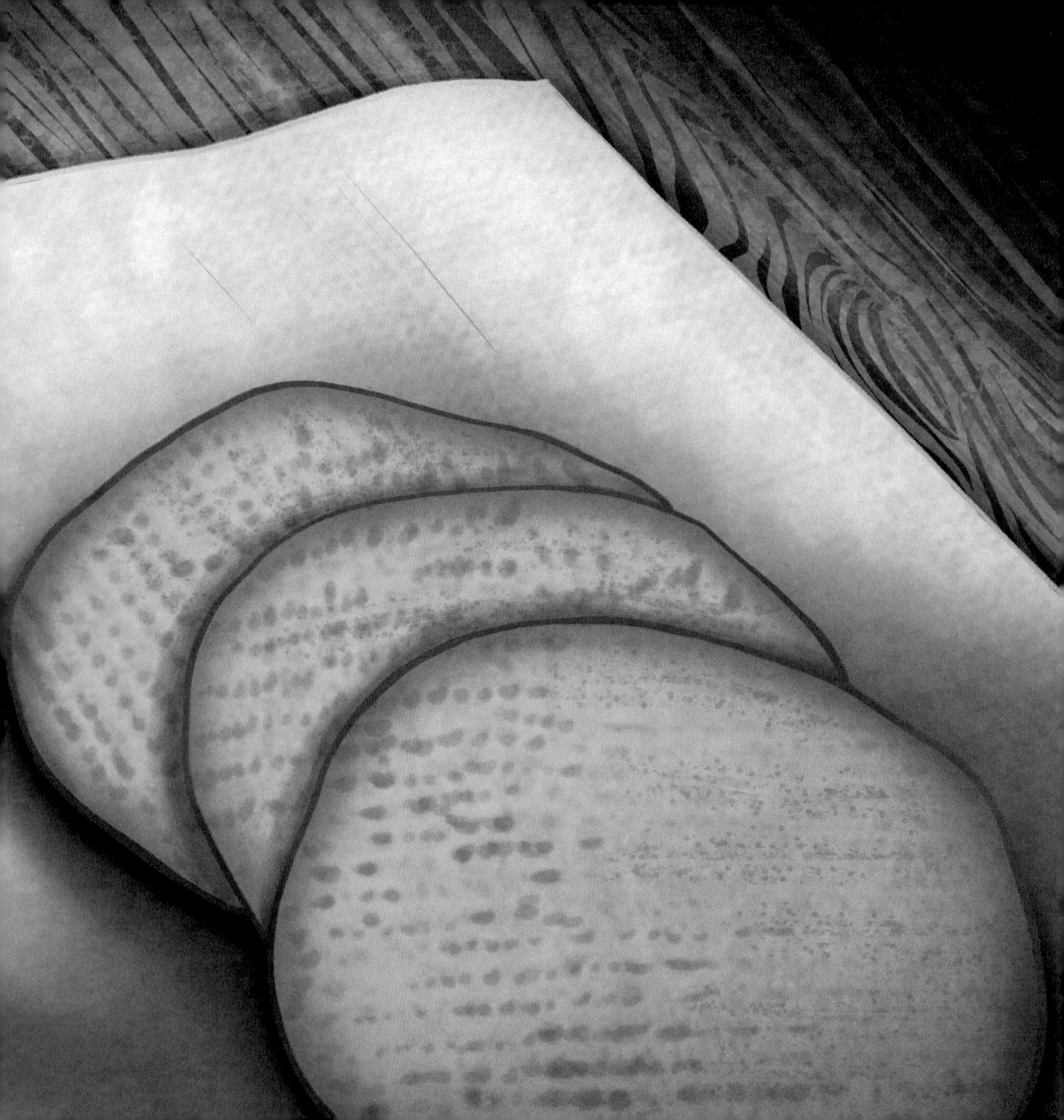

Mark's Gospel
STUDY #23

Missing the Point

📖 **Read:** Mark 8:10-21

💬 **Talk:**

1. Do you like sandwiches? Two pieces of bread with something yummy in between them? Mark 8:1-21 is like a sandwich. It begins and ends describing how Jesus fed a lot of people with physical food. The truth we are to see is that Jesus is the provider and satisfier that people truly need. Let's look at how everyone misses the point.

2. The Pharisees (vs11-13) demanded a sign from Jesus that He was truly the Messiah *right after* Jesus performed this miracle. Do you think they asked because they believed from their hearts that He was Messiah? *[no, they wanted to trick or shame Jesus]*

3. The Disciples (vs14-21) forgot to bring enough food and they thought Jesus was disappointed with them. But was Jesus upset about having enough food? *[no]*

- Jesus was more concerned about the Pharisees' heart-attitude. They did not think they needed God or Jesus, because they were righteous all on their own. Spiritual self-reliance is a proud attitude that rejects God. In which verse does Jesus warn the disciples about this attitude? *[v15]*

4. The Point of Jesus' illustration: While Jesus satisfied people's stomachs with a miracle, it points to the fact that only Jesus can satisfy our hearts and souls. Many people in Jesus' day were self-reliant. The religious leaders didn't think they were hungry, spiritually speaking, but in truth they were starved. The Romans (Herod) were also proud and self-reliant. But to Whom should we look to provide the needs of our hearts and our physical life? *[God alone]*

5. So, while the disciples could see and hear just fine (v18), their souls were still blind and deaf. They were still missing the point of Jesus' miracles and preaching.

❤️ **Pray:** Lord, open our eyes to Your truth and our ears to Your Word. When our hearts are sad, Jesus satisfies. When we steal or lie and feel badly, Jesus forgives and satisfies. Thank you for Jesus' death on the cross that took away our guilt and shame and placed it all on Jesus. Truly, Jesus is the satisfier that people truly need.

🎵 **Sing:** "Come, Christians, Join to Sing" - We will sing His praises for all eternity, what a great Savior! (pg 99)

⇉ EXTRA TIME? ⇇
Go make a sandwich and discuss how Mark's Gospel will sandwich a very important truth in the middle of two events in Jesus' ministry. Then, enjoy the snack!

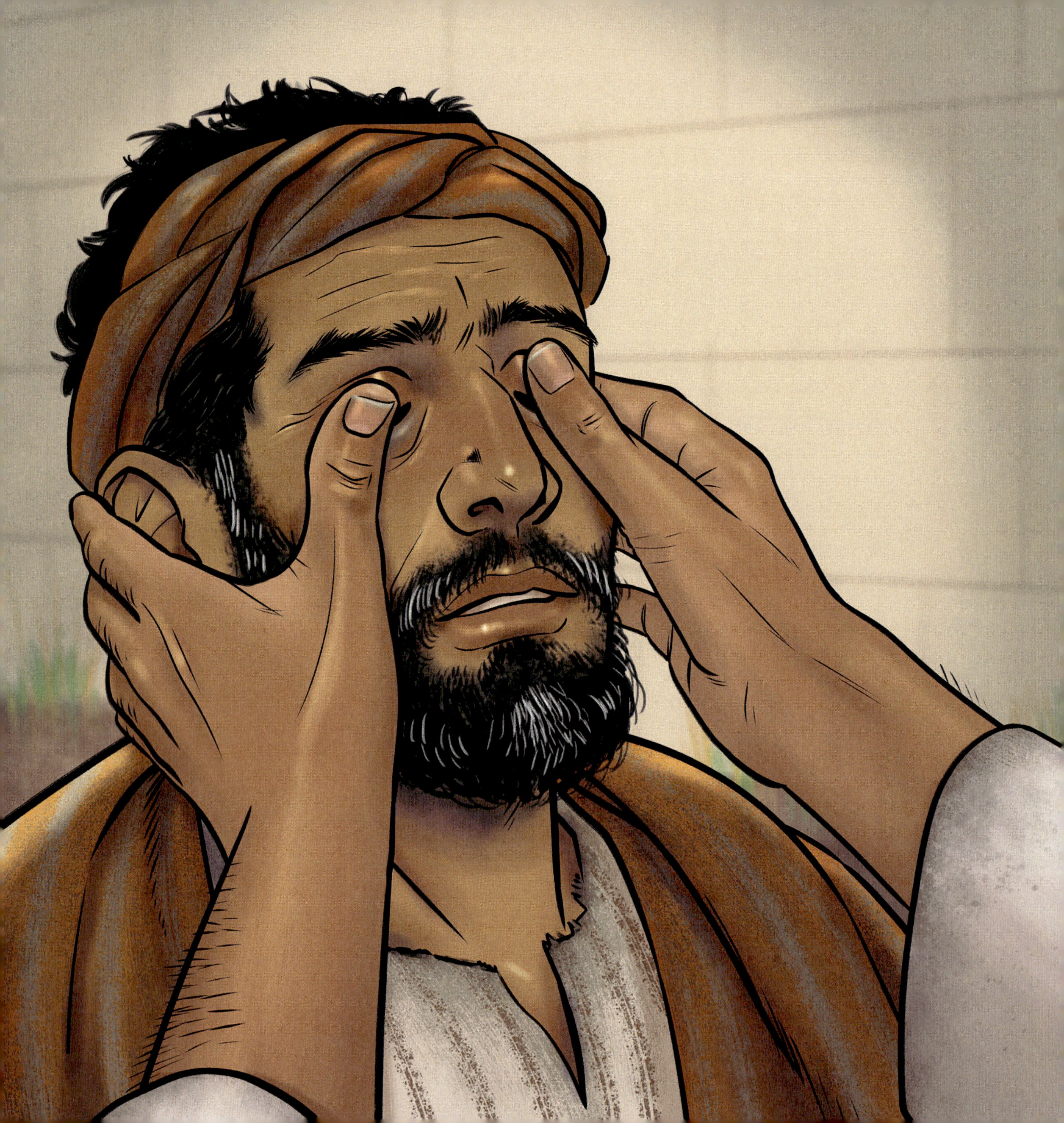

Mark's Gospel
STUDY #24

Seeing Clearly

📖 **Read:** Mark 8:22-33

💬 **Talk:**

1. In the last study, Jesus pointed out that the disciples are missing the point. They did not fully understand the kind of Messiah that Jesus is. They had their own ideas what the Messiah, God's promised salvation, would be like. The study today pictures that misunderstanding with the illustration of eyesight.

2. Where did Jesus take the blind man in this passage? (v23) *[outside the village of Bethsaida]* What is different about this healing? *[the man couldn't see clearly the first time]* So what did Jesus do? (v25) *[Jesus laid His hands on the man again]*

3. Do not misunderstand this passage! The man did not have blurry vision the first time because Jesus' power somehow failed, or that the man did not have enough faith. Jesus only partially healed the man as a picture, an illustration, of the spiritual blindness of the disciples and Jewish people.

4. Connect this study in your mind with Study #23. It is about seeing clearly. Did the disciples fully understand Who Jesus was? *[no]* No, they didn't.

5. The disciples *knew* Jesus was the Messiah, the Christ. (vs27-30) But in a spiritual way, their vision was still blurry. *They had their own ideas* what Messiah would be like. They expected and wanted a strong and conquering king.

6. But the Messiah God had in mind to rescue sinners was Jesus, the suffering servant of God. (v31) If the disciples were seeing clearly, they would have understood this about Jesus.

- But to reveal their spiritual vision was still blurry, Mark shares with us how Peter argued with Jesus (vs32-33). Jesus strongly scolds Peter for arguing against God's will and His rescue plan to save the souls of mankind.

❤️ **Pray:** Father, how patient You are with us! Even when we begin to understand Your ways and Your will, sometimes our view is cloudy and blurry. Again, we pray that You would open our eyes to Your Word so that we may understand Your ways. Thank You for giving us Your Word that helps us see just how blind we can be. Thank You for Your immeasurable patience, kindness, and love.

🎵 **Sing:** "Come, Christians, Join to Sing"" is a fitting song for this study. (pg 99)

> **⇉ BEING JESUS' DISCIPLE MEANS UNDERSTANDING ⇇**
> Any disciple of Jesus who wants to understand Jesus must humbly accept Who Jesus is.

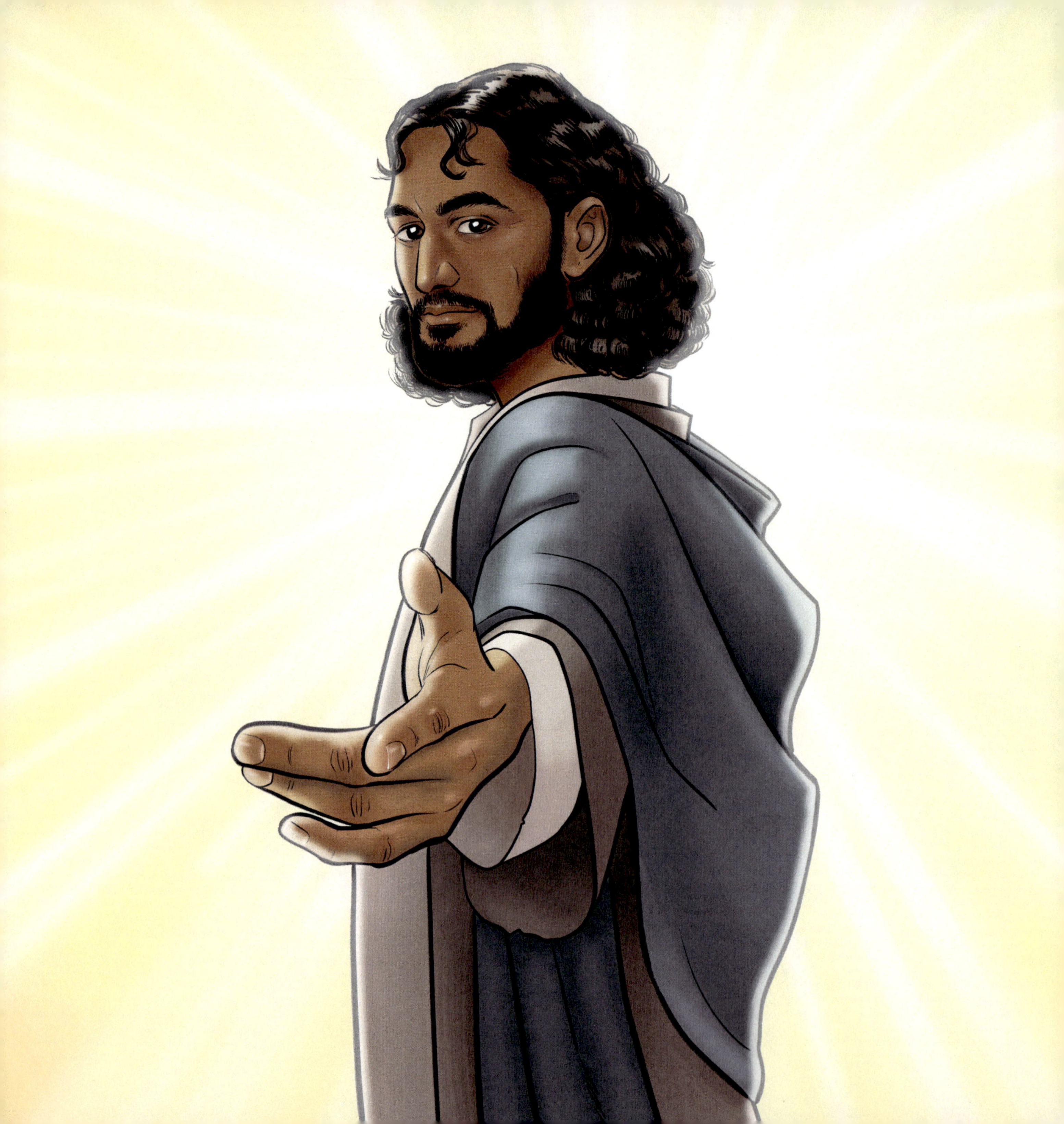

Mark's Gospel
STUDY #25

High Prices

📖 **Read:** Mark 8:34-38

💬 **Talk:**

1. Have you ever been excited to buy something, maybe a toy or candy, but when you found out the price you were less excited? No doubt the adults in the store have said, "No, we're not buying that, it's too expensive!" Sometimes we desire something enough that we're willing to pay the high price because we think it is worth the sacrifice.

2. V35 is talking about life in this present world and life after this one, eternity. Jesus makes several statements that sound confusing, as if they contradict each other. But here is what they mean:

   - Whoever lives in a self-centered way in this present world - thinking they are saving their life - will not actually have eternal life with God. This means that in the end, they will lose the life and peace they wanted to keep.

   - However, those who give up a self-centered, rebellious life in this present world - knowingly giving it to God - will actually find eternal peace and relationship with God. This is what is called eternal life.

   - Eternal life is only found through Jesus Christ, God's Son.

3. The first half of the Gospel of Mark has focused on "Being God's Servant and Disciple". Before moving to the second half of the book, Mark includes this passage to clearly teach us that following Jesus requires personal sacrifice. Some people decide the price is too high and do not follow the Lord. Other people decide that Jesus is too valuable and willingly pay any price to follow Him.

4. Mark included this passage because Jesus is asking you this question too. Jesus isn't asking for money. He's asking for your heart and for your life. What He offers in return is eternal life in Him. Is the price too high for you to pay?

❤️ **Pray:** God, You gave Your only Son to die a death He didn't deserve and rescue rebellious sinners like us. When we consider the cost of following You, Your Word is true and Your name is worthy of our worship, and our lives, and our all.

🎵 **Sing:** "I Have Decided" (pg 104)   Also, "All I Have is Christ" (not included in hymn section).

⇒ BEING JESUS' DISCIPLE MEANS SACRIFICE ⇐
Anything sacrificed on earth doesn't compare to heaven. Live with an eternal mindset.

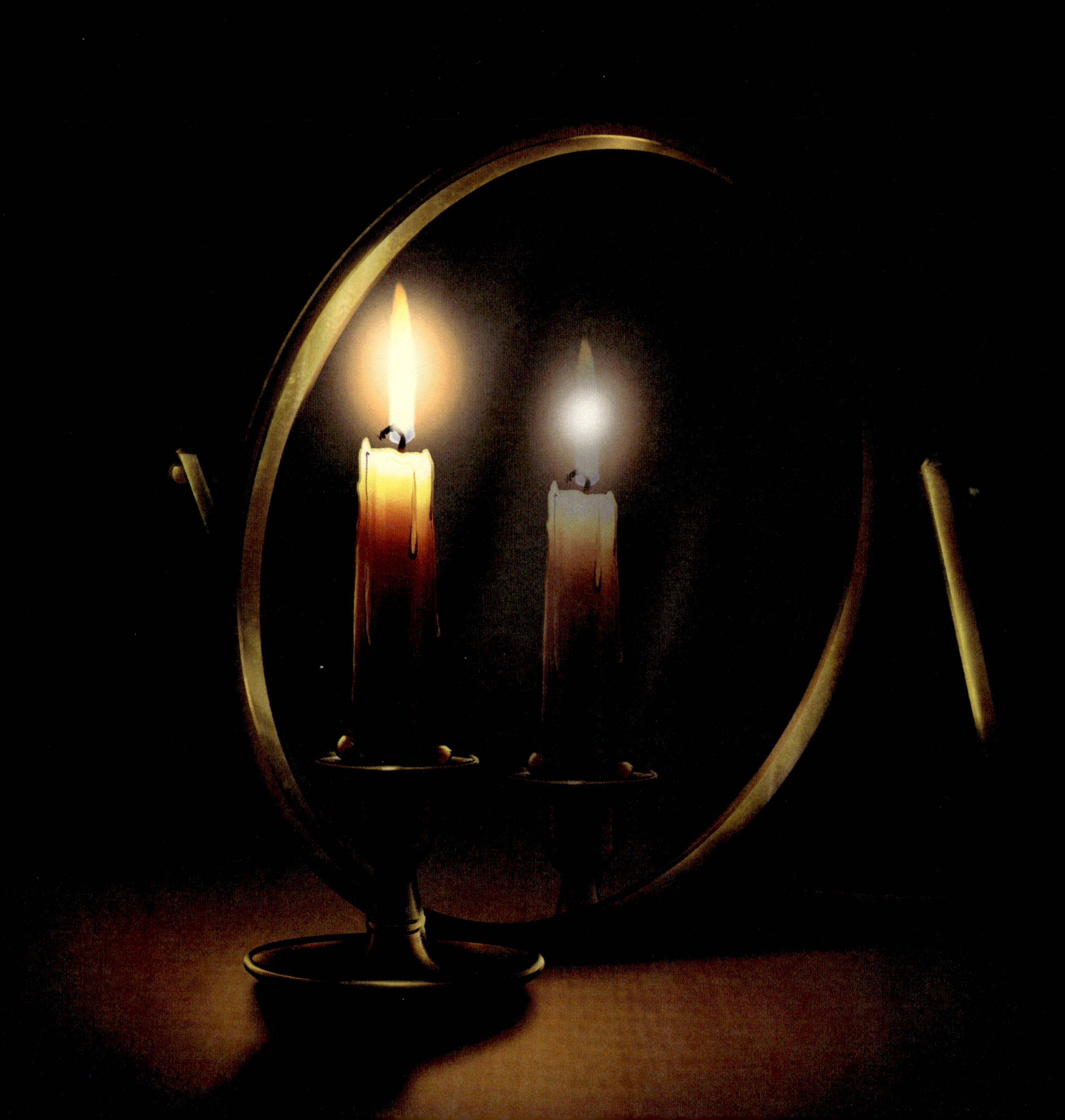

Mark's Gospel
STUDY #26

Jesus Reveals His Glory

📖 **Read:** Mark 9:1-13

💬 **Talk:**

1. Imagine you are standing in a dark room. You light a candle and the room is lit with flickering light. The candle is a source of light. Now, what if you were to place that candle in front of a mirror? While the light in the room gets brighter, does this mean that the mirror is a source of light too? *[no, it only reflects light]*

2. Who did Jesus take up the mountain with Him? *[Peter, James and John]*

3. What does "transfigured" mean? *[that Jesus' glory was revealed, and His appearance was changed in front of the disciples for a time]*

   - In today's passage we see that Jesus' glory and light comes *from Himself* because He is God. When Moses and Elijah were there with Jesus, the brightness from their clothing was like that mirror - *a reflection* of the glory of God.

   - Before Jesus came, people listened to God's Word through Moses and Elijah (Law and Prophets). But now Jesus - as the beloved Son - is presented as superior to them. Being Jesus' disciple means listening to Him (v7).

4. Read what Peter said in vs5-6. Afraid and confused, Peter blurts out an offer to make a tent for each of the three people in front of him, similar to hospitality in the Old Testament for prophets. You see, at this point in Jesus' ministry, the disciples *still* did not understand that Jesus was God. Peter offered to put tents together for Moses and Elijah, but Jesus was not just a prophet of Jehovah, He IS God.

5. When Peter saw Jesus' clothes shining "whiter than any clothes, ever" was Jesus the *source* of the light (like the candle) or a *reflection* of God's glory (like the mirror)? *[Jesus' own glory was revealed on that mountain because He is God]*

6. Do you think that Peter, James and John did not fully understand what they saw until after Jesus rose from the dead? (vs9-10) *[yes, they probably did not fully understand]*

❤️ **Pray:** Heavenly Father, one day we will enjoy Your presence and glory. While it may be a blessing to meet the people we read about in Scripture, we look forward the most to seeing You face to face!

🎵 **Sing:** "Crown Him with Many Crowns" (pg 101)

⇾ EXTRA TIME? ⇽

Try entering a dark room with your family and bring a mirror and a light source (flashlight, candle, etc). As you test different combinations of light and mirrors to light the room, be sure to make the point that Jesus is the Light of the world (John 1:4-5; John 8:12).

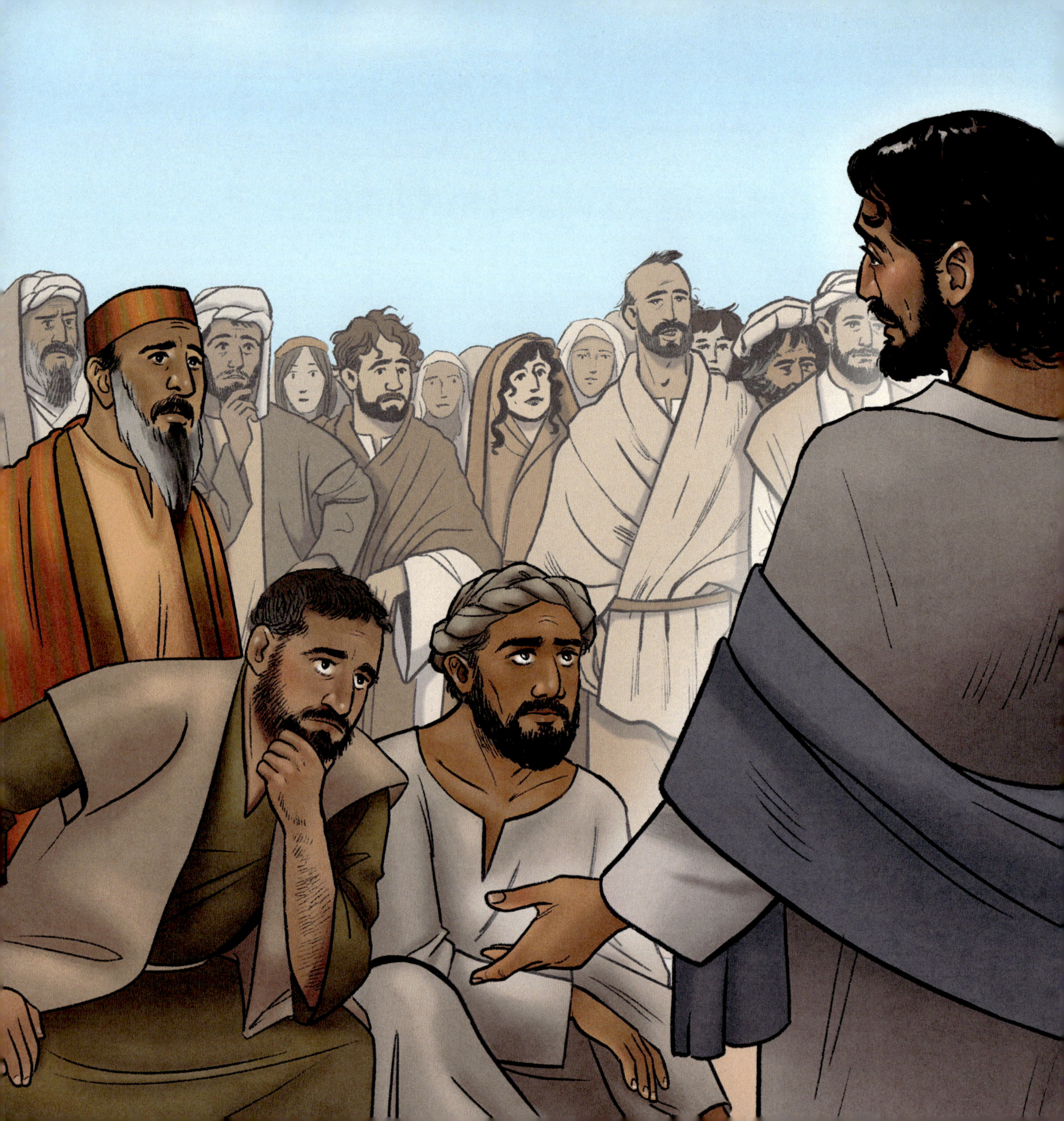

Mark's Gospel
STUDY #27

Divine Help

📖 **Read:** Mark 9:14-29

💬 **Talk:**

1. In your life, when do you look for help? When the item is too heavy, when you are stuck, when there is danger, when you cannot figure out a problem - you look for help at those times, right? *[yes]* In this study we see that God alone has power to help!

2. The father's unsteady belief that **God alone can help**:
   - Vs21-24 are not teaching that you can have anything you want if you only believe. We learn that divine help is available for any need if we believe! Sometimes we believe and struggle with unbelief at the same time.
   - Often our faith can be misplaced, trusting in anything other than Jesus. We have faith in ourselves, our bank accounts, the government, our health or something else. We fail to believe the promises of God's Word, or to pray in faith for the fulfillment of those promises.
   - Here's what Jesus is saying: "It's not a question of whether I can do it, but will you believe I can do it, for everything is possible for him who believes."
   - Faith is about the Object (God) and it grows when we focus more on Jesus than our circumstances.

3. The disciple's unbelief that **God alone can help**:
   - In vs28-29, the disciples ask Jesus why they could not cast the demon out. Do you remember that Jesus gave them authority to preach and cast out demons earlier? (Mark 6:7)
   - What is Jesus' answer to their question? (v29) *[prayer is necessary for driving out stubborn spirits]*
   - Truth for Today: Both faith and prayer testify that spiritual power is not in oneself but in God alone, and both wait in trust upon His promise to save.
   - Jesus taught everyone there that God alone has power to help!

❤️ **Pray:** Father, much of our lives are beyond our control. We cannot control our health, our livelihood, or even the date of our death. All things are in Your holy, powerful hands. Teach us to turn to You early in our problems, not to ourselves first. Teach us to faithfully wait on You until Your help is given.

🎵 **Sing:** "Fairest Lord Jesus" (pg 102)

⇋ BEING JESUS' DISCIPLE MEANS DEPENDENCE ⇌
The best circumstances for your heart are those situations where it is obvious God alone can help you.

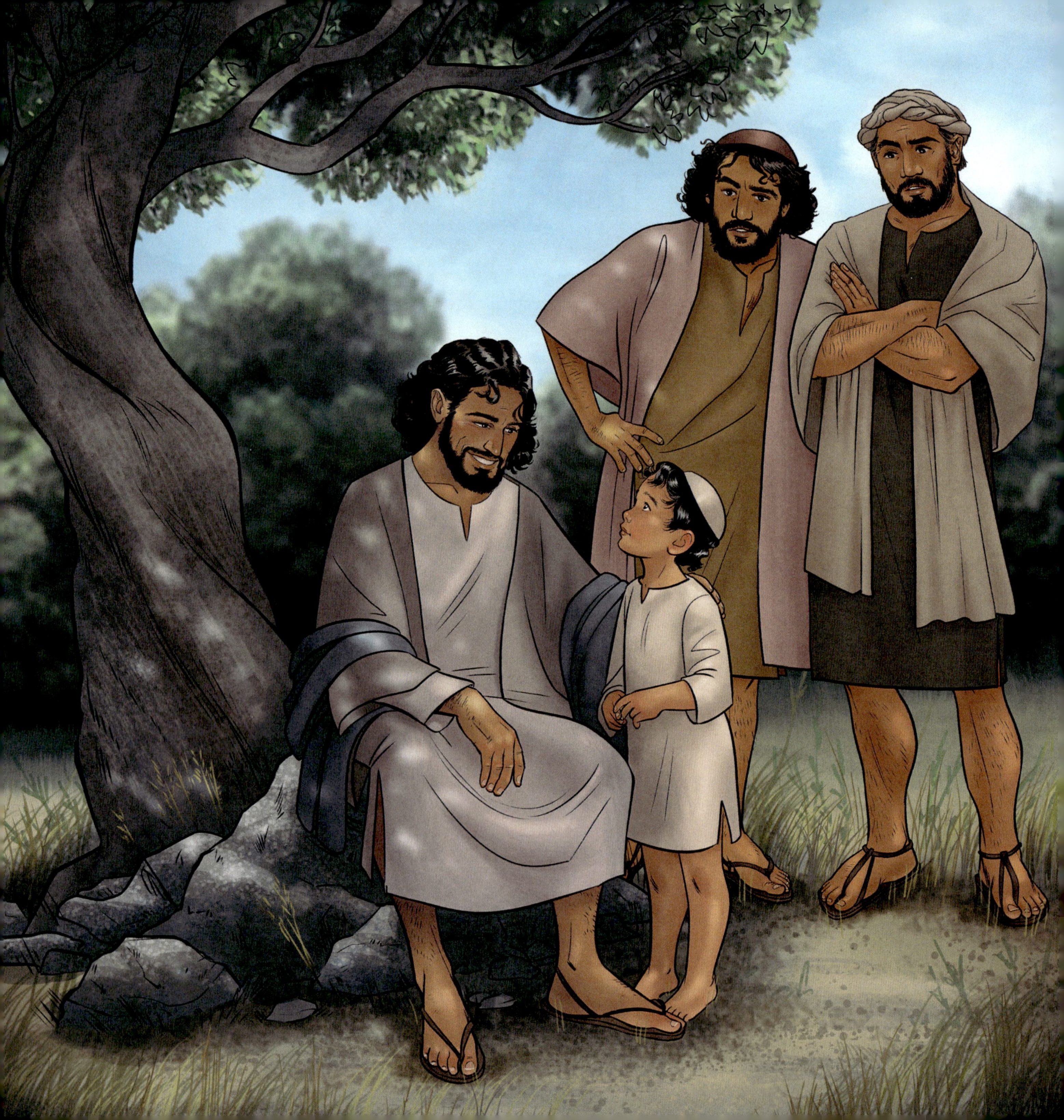

Mark's Gospel
STUDY #28

Jesus Teaches: 1/5 "On Discipleship"

📖 **Read:** Mark 9:30-50 (Section is from Mark 9:30 - 11:25)

💬 **Talk:**

1. Go back to Mark 8:34 and read it. Now, read again Mark 9:31. Do you think Jesus has called His disciples to do more than He was willing to do? *[no]* In this passage, Jesus teaches us that obeying God may have an earthly cost, but also a high eternal gain.

2. What were the disciples arguing about in v34? *[who would be greatest]* Does everyone tend to be proud and think themselves more important than they should? *[yes]* A humble disciple of Jesus will be found caring for the very people that the world doesn't care about. They won't be thinking about humility; the disciple of Jesus will not be thinking of themselves at all. **In this passage, Jesus teaches us that His disciple will not fight for status and importance, but will care for even the lowest and unnoticed person.**

3. Vs38-41: When the disciples tried to discourage someone from casting out demons in Jesus' name, how did Jesus respond? (v39) *[don't stop him]* Did John expect Jesus to thank him or rebuke him? *[thank him]* **In this passage, Jesus teaches us that His disciples do not compete with other believers who are not in their group.** As Jesus' disciples, pride will not help us accomplish God's work for us. Pride only divides believers into groups that fight each other. If someone is truly preaching Christ, do not stop them simply because you do not know them.

4. In vs42-50, what does Jesus say a person should remove from their body if that body part causes them to sin? *[hand, foot, eye]* We know that Jesus doesn't mean for people to *actually* do that, because scripture tells us that the body isn't the source of sin - the heart is (Romans 6:13). **In this passage, Jesus gives a strong warning to all His disciples who mistreat others and lead them to disbelief and sin.**

❤️ **Pray:** Heavenly Father, we study the life of Jesus and we see Your humble Servant Who did everything You asked perfectly. Help us learn humility and promote the gospel on Your terms, not our own. May we learn to love You more than anything else we love. Thank You for Your Word that patiently and clearly teaches us.

🎵 **Sing:** "Trust and Obey" in response to this section on Jesus' Teaching. (pg 111)

⇾ EXTRA TIME? ⇽

Think about the people in your church or community. Who are the people that aren't noticed very much? How about the people who no one talks to or befriends? In Jesus day, children were overlooked and undervalued. In our day, Jesus gives us the example of reaching out to the people the world ignores. Who might that be in your life? Talk as a family about it.

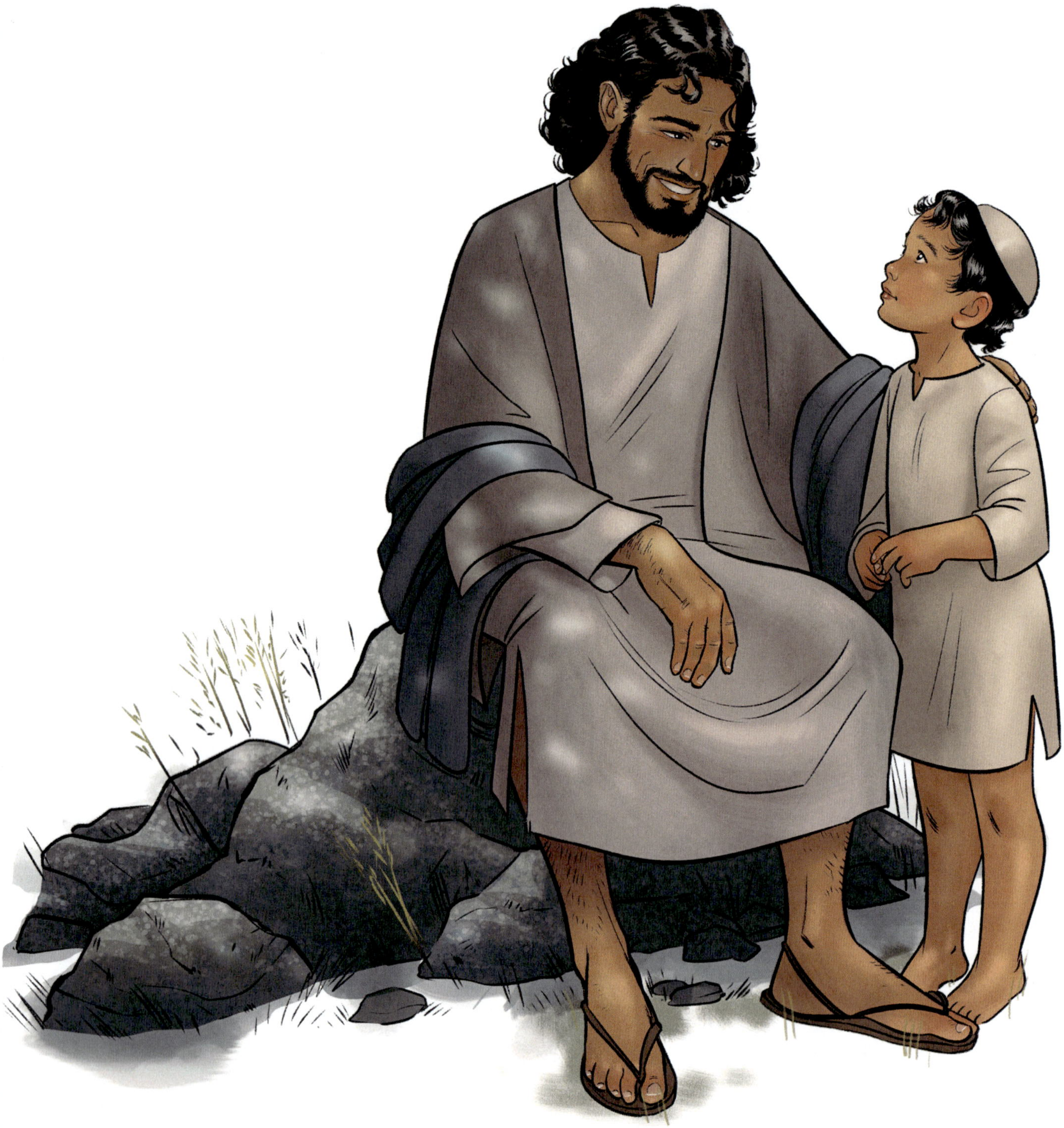

Mark's Gospel
STUDY #29

Jesus Teaches: 2/5 "On Family"

📖 **Read:** Mark 10:1-16 (Section is from Mark 9:30 - 11:25)

💬 **Talk:**

1. The world is not as it should be, is it? What are some things in the world today that are not good, right, or fair? *[allow answers]* There are many hurtful things that happen in life that cause us to turn to God.

2. **In this passage, Jesus teaches that our focus should be on the blessing of marriage as God designed it.** The Pharisees tried to find fault in Jesus' teaching on the law of Moses. What is divorce? *[when a married man and woman declare in court that they are no longer married]* The world isn't as it should be. Even in a broken world, God puts boundaries on our suffering (God's regulation on divorce through Moses), but the ideal relationship for marriage is God's original design. The Pharisees only wanted to argue about rules and catching Jesus in His words.

3. Have you ever had a bug fly around your head and follow you? *[no doubt, yes]* You were trying to do something else and the bug wouldn't leave you alone! The disciples felt that way about the children that came to see Jesus.

- To be fair, in the 1st century children were not very important in the culture until they became adults. However, **in this passage Jesus teaches that children are equally important as adults and receive Jesus' attention and love.**

- As a child, if you have people in your life that love you and teach you to come to Jesus in faith, you are very blessed! The adults who are studying God's Word with you right now are a blessing to you. Even if no one were to want you around, you have Jesus Christ - He loves you and knows you. He created you unique. You are fearfully and wonderfully made (Psalm 139).

- In response? Live for the One Who values you. Adore Jesus. He did not "stop what He was doing" in order to spend time with children. Blessing the children was exactly what the Father wanted Jesus to do that day! Jesus' work that day *was* the children.

❤️ **Pray:** God in heaven, You made a perfect world that sin - even our own sin - continues to ruin. Help us to look to You and Your Word for the answers to life's tough questions. Give us Your point of view on the people around us. It is too easy for us to be annoyed with others instead of seeing eternal souls that need the gospel. Thank you for Jesus' love and care for the small and overlooked people of the world.

🎵 **Sing:** "Trust and Obey" in response to this section on Jesus' Teaching. (pg 111)

⇒ BEING JESUS' DISCIPLE MEANS TRUSTING WHEN LIFE HURTS ⇐

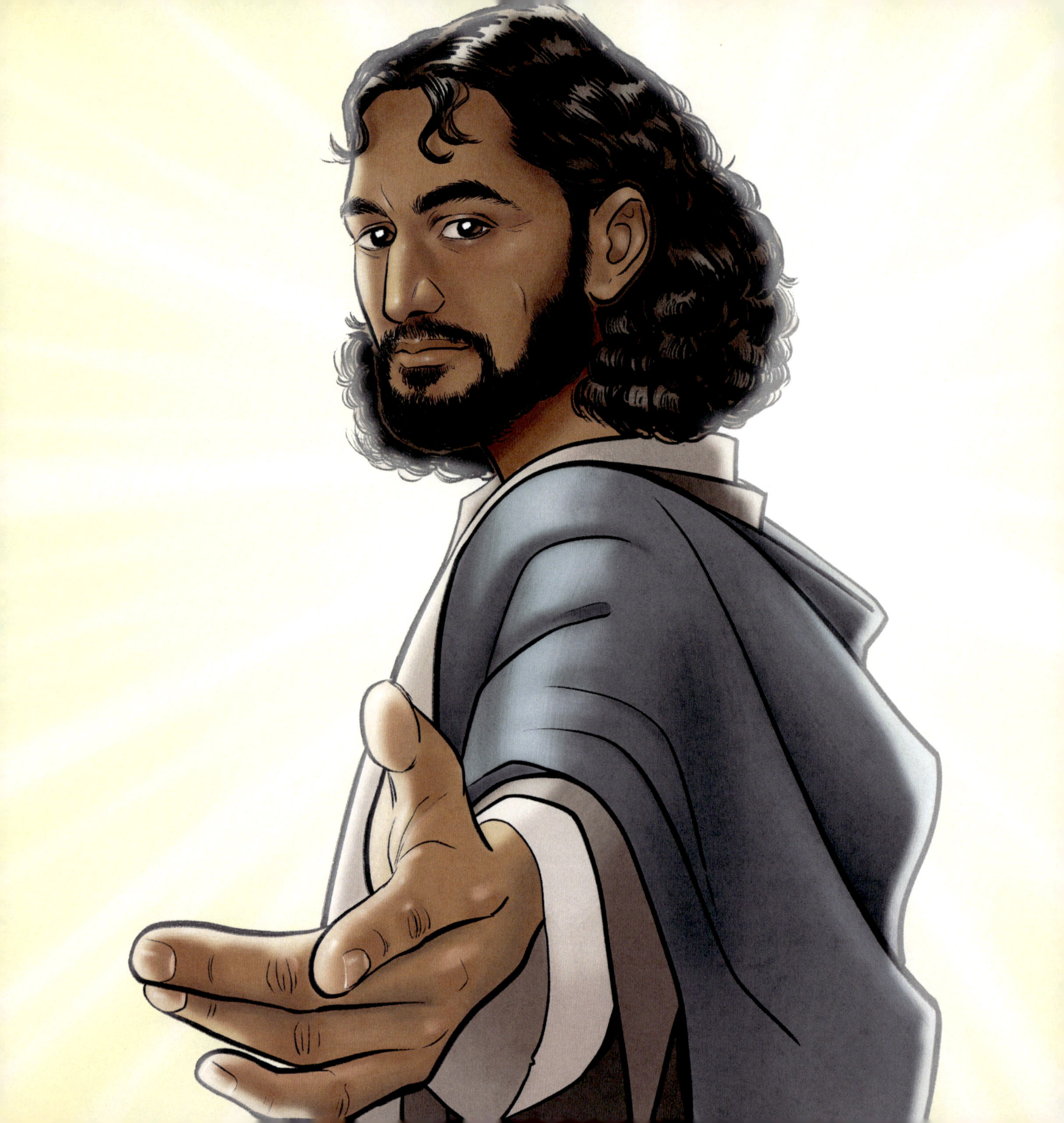

Mark's Gospel
STUDY #30
Jesus Teaches: 3/5 "On Wealth"

📖 **Read:** Mark 10:17-31 (Section is from Mark 9:30 - 11:25)

💬 **Talk:** "I don't need anyone. I can take care of myself!"

1. Self-sufficiency and pride are celebrated in some cultures, but that kind of statement should not be in the heart and mind of a disciple of Jesus.

2. The young man thought he had done everything right, like the apostle Paul (Philippians 3:6). Self-righteousness is believing you're good enough to please God. What examples of self-righteousness does Jesus give in v19? *[read]* Did the rich young ruler think he did all these things the way God commanded? *[yes, he thought so]*

3. Do you think Jesus is teaching that owning things is wrong? *[no, owning things is not evil]* Loving what you own more than God is evil. Everything we own should be yielded to God. "Yielded" means that whatever God gives or removes from us does not change our attitude of love for God.

- What is your favorite possession? A toy? A pet? Your home? *[allow response]* Is that thing "yielded" to God? Would you love God just the same even without that favorite possession?

4. Our possessions are not really ours. Do you remember the story of Joseph? What was his job in Egypt when he was a slave? *[in charge of Potiphar's household]* Joseph was a steward. The things he cared for day after day were not really his, but Potiphar's. In a similar way, the things we "own" aren't ours, but God's.

5. Vs29-30 may *appear* to say that Christians will receive a lot of material possessions in this life as reward for making sacrifices for Jesus. But that isn't true. **In this passage, Jesus is teaching us that when we loosen our grip on "my stuff" for Christ's sake, 1) we gain dependence** on God to provide for us, **2) we have fellowship** with other believers, and **3) we share** with one another. Today, we also gain a new and spiritual family in the church.

6. We need God for everything. Be humble enough to admit that truth!

❤️ **Pray:** Father, the world and everything in it is Yours, including us. You made us and we have not made ourselves. Whether You give us many earthly possessions or few, give us the wisdom to steward them well so that the world may more clearly see Who You are and what You are like!

🎵 **Sing:** "Trust and Obey" in response to this section on Jesus' Teaching. (pg 111)

⇒ EXTRA TIME? ⇐

Look up the following verses and discuss how they reveal the rich young ruler's heart. Exodus 20:3 (money was his god), Luke 16:13 (serving God and riches), Proverbs 15:16 (he would be better off loving God more than anything, including his riches)

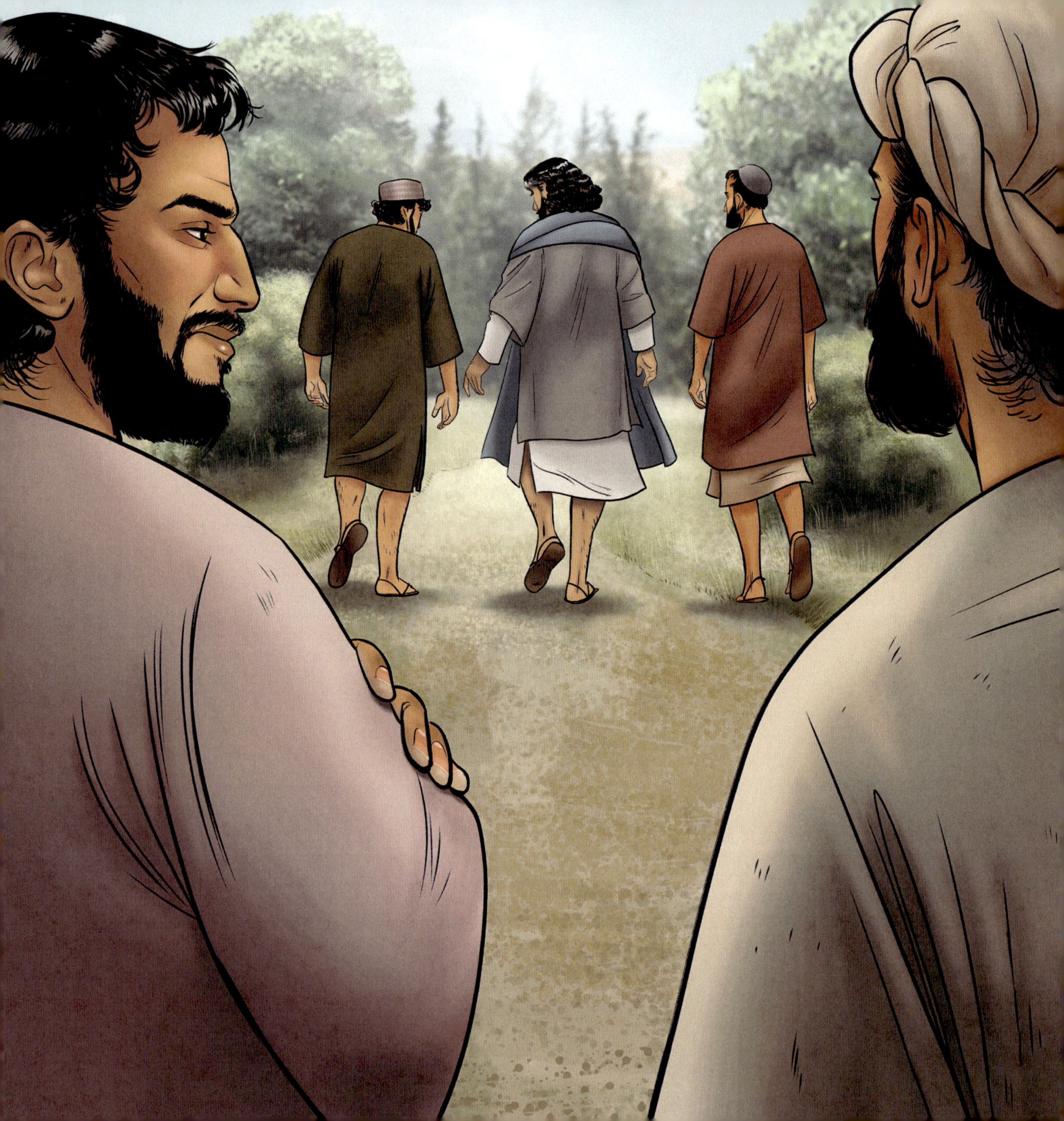

Mark's Gospel
—— STUDY #31 ——
Jesus Teaches: 4/5 "On Humility"

📖 **Read:** Mark 10:32-52 (Section is from Mark 9:30 - 11:25)

💬 **Talk:**

1. In vs32-34, Jesus is on His way to Jerusalem. The disciples and the crowd are amazed at Jesus' serious determination to go to Jerusalem. Why? *[because they know the danger Jesus will face from the religious leaders there]*

2. After Jesus warns them of His suffering and death, what do James and John ask from Jesus? *[to sit next to Him in the kingdom]* Sitting next to a ruler was a place of honor and trust. Mark includes these verses to tell us that the disciples *still did not understand* what kind of Messiah God had sent to them.

3. Vs42-45: Name a ruler or king that was a very severe, cruel leader. From your history lessons, can you think of any? *[allow responses]*

   - For the world system, leadership means being the boss, and everyone has to obey the boss. Often, people accept a severe leader for promises of safety or comfort.

   - For God's kingdom, leadership means what? (v43) *[being a servant]*

   - Jesus is the world's very best leader, but He served other people and obeyed God completely. Can you think of some ways He showed this? *[answers will vary - washing disciples' feet, healing others even when tired, etc.]*

4. The longer the disciples were with Jesus, the more their spiritual blindness was being healed. Mark includes the healing of Bartimaeus in this passage as the final healing miracle of Jesus before He enters Jerusalem for Passover celebration.

5. What kind of spiritual pride might be blinding you from seeing Jesus clearly? Have you ever thought of that? All of us struggle with pride - it just looks different for each person. Has God used these studies in Mark to bring to your mind the pride or spiritual blindness in your life?

❤️ **Pray:** Father, open our eyes to Your Word and to our sin. Help us fight our pride and admit our need for a Redeemer. Pride keeps us all from seeing You clearly and coming to You in faith. Thank You for Jesus' patience - with His disciples then and with us today.

🎵 **Sing:** "Trust and Obey" in response to this section on Jesus' Teaching. (pg 111)

⇉ EXTRA TIME? ⇇
Grab a pen and paper. Write out five proud statements that children might say about themselves to make other people think they are great, talented, and wonderful. Now think about Jesus' humility and write out the ways a disciple of Christ should talk and think in those same situations. Sometimes it isn't helpful to just point out what pride is. We also need to think about what humility thinks and does.

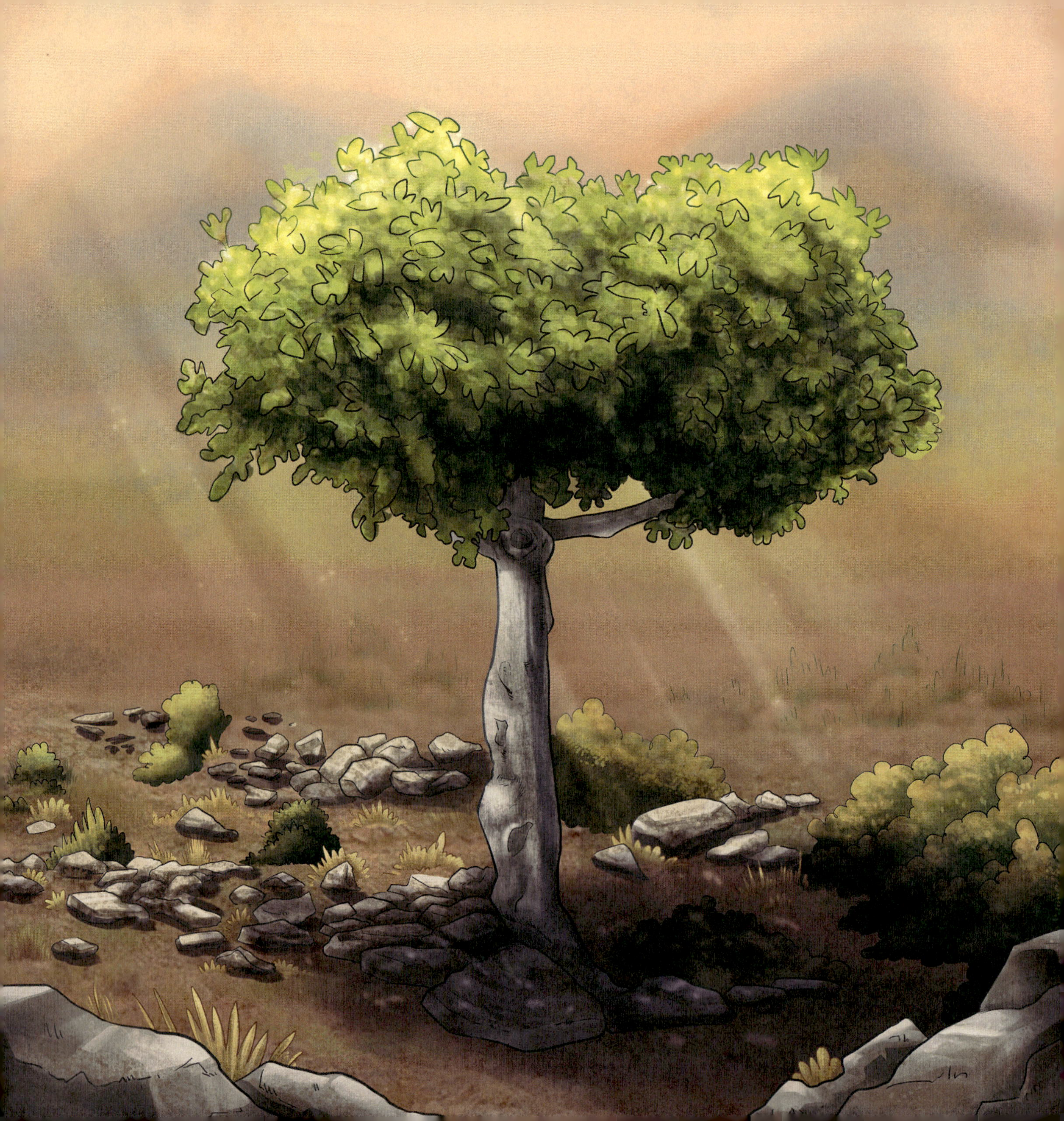

Mark's Gospel
— STUDY #32 —

Jesus Teaches: 5/5 "On Genuine Faith"

📖 **Read:** Mark 11:1-14 & 11:20-25 (Section is from Mark 9:30 - 11:25)

💬 **Talk:**

1. It was the time of Passover and Jerusalem had many travelers who hoped to celebrate together in the next few days. Jesus knew what would happen at the end of the week but proceeded to Jerusalem anyway, because it was God's Plan.

2. Read Zechariah 9:9. Did Jesus fulfill this prophecy about Messiah? *[yes]*

3. The excitement and cheering of the crowd as Jesus entered Jerusalem was genuine. Sadly, the people *still did not understand* what kind of Messiah Jesus, God's suffering Servant, would be. They still expected a conquering king. (v10) Their excitement turned to anger less than a week later when they discovered that Jesus would not set up the kingdom they wanted. Which kingdom was ruling the world at this time? *[Roman Empire]*

4. As people cheered Jesus riding into the city, did they really understand what they were doing? *[no]*

5. Vs12-14; 20-25 - When Jesus cursed the fig tree, do you think 1) He was upset that there was no fruit, so He cursed the tree? 2) He was teaching the disciples a spiritual lesson? Or 3) Jesus didn't like figs anyway? *[#2]*

- **Lesson**: As Jesus preached to the Jewish people for three years, their hearts had the leafy appearance of a healthy tree that should have had fruit. However, all their religiosity was for show with no tender attitude toward God.

- **Lesson**: Jesus had real fruit and genuine faith in God; He challenges us to follow His example. Jesus showed us what happens when a child of God lives in a close relationship with God. Jesus lived every moment of the day close to God and His 'fruit' was real. Jesus trusted His Father in the right way for all the right things and for all the right reasons.

❤️ **Pray:** God, it is easier to see the empty, religious pride of the religious leaders and the people in Jesus' day. It is much more difficult to see our own proud sin. Help us leave our pride and trust You in faith. As we seek You, we know we will find You and begin to see life and the world the same way Jesus does. Help our faith to be genuine!

🎵 **Sing:** "Trust and Obey". (pg 111)   Also, "Wonderful, Merciful Savior" (not included in hymn section).

⇉ EXTRA TIME? ⇇

The fig tree was a regular illustration for Israel (Jeremiah 8:13, Hosea 9:10,16). Not only had Jesus preached to them for 3 years, but God had long endured with Israel while they rejected the prophets over the centuries, and eventually his own Son. Discuss who some of these prophets were and how they were rejected.

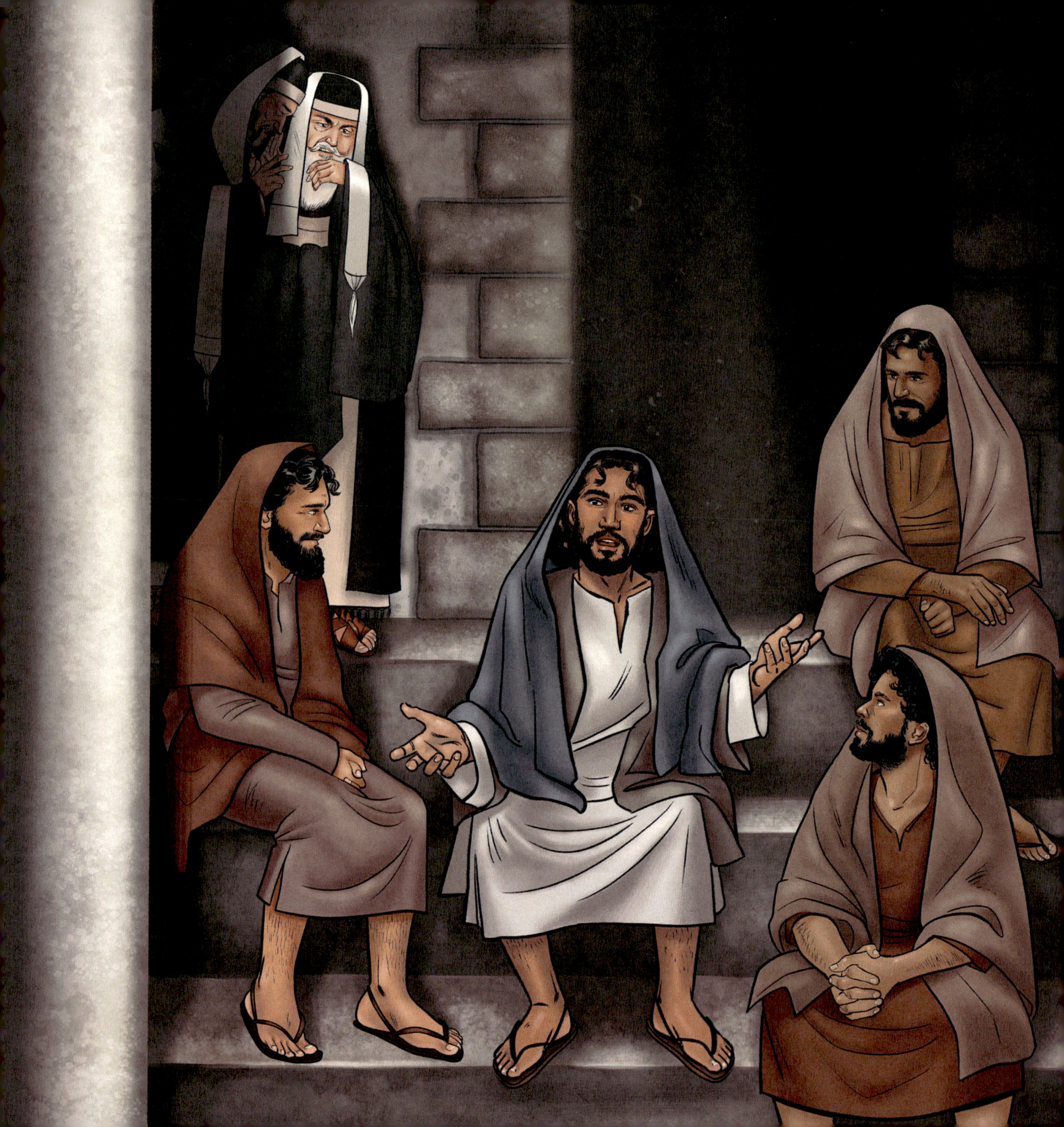

Mark's Gospel
STUDY #33

Jesus' Authority: 1/5 "The Temple"

📖 **Read:** Mark 11:15-19 & 11:27-33 (Section is from Mark 11:15 - 12:44)

💬 **Talk:**

1. **Imagine**: Thousands of people in Jerusalem for the Passover celebration. The Jewish people had celebrated Passover since the time God delivered Israel from Egypt over 1,000 years before. Many would compare deliverance from Egypt at the first Passover to Jesus entering Jerusalem to free them from Rome. "Put yourself in their shoes" as you study what Jesus did during the week leading up to the cross on Calvary. What might the people have been thinking?

2. Read vs15-16. What did Jesus stop from happening within the temple? *[selling of animals, changing money/currencies]* In the outer courts of the temple, Gentiles who had converted to Judaism were allowed to worship. This outer court was where the animals were being sold.

3. When Jesus chased out the money changers and animals, the chief priests realized that their own authority was being confronted by Jesus. Who do you think allowed all the merchants in the temple courtyard? *[the chief priests]* And who said they shouldn't be there? *[Jesus]* So what was the question asked of Jesus in v28? *[who gave You the authority?]*

4. This section is about Jesus' authority as God versus the priest's authority. Who did the priests fear? *[v32-the people]* Whose will did Jesus obey? *[God's will]*

5. For the next four studies, we will see how Jesus' authority made the religious leaders jealous and very angry. They felt so threatened that they looked for ways to have Him killed. While this was an evil intention, did God use it for good? *[yes]* How? *[by providing a way for salvation and rescue through God's perfect Lamb, Jesus Christ]*

❤️ **Pray:** Father, help us to see Your authority in this world and in our lives. We see how sinful our hearts can be when Jesus reveals His authority. Help us to yield our will to You. When the decision is Your way or ours, we want to choose Your way.

🎵 **Sing:** "Jesus Shall Reign". (pg 106)   Also, "O Great God" (not included in hymn section).

⇾ BEING JESUS' DISCIPLE MEANS SUBMISSION ⇽
A disciple of Jesus submits (willingly obeys) to God's authority.

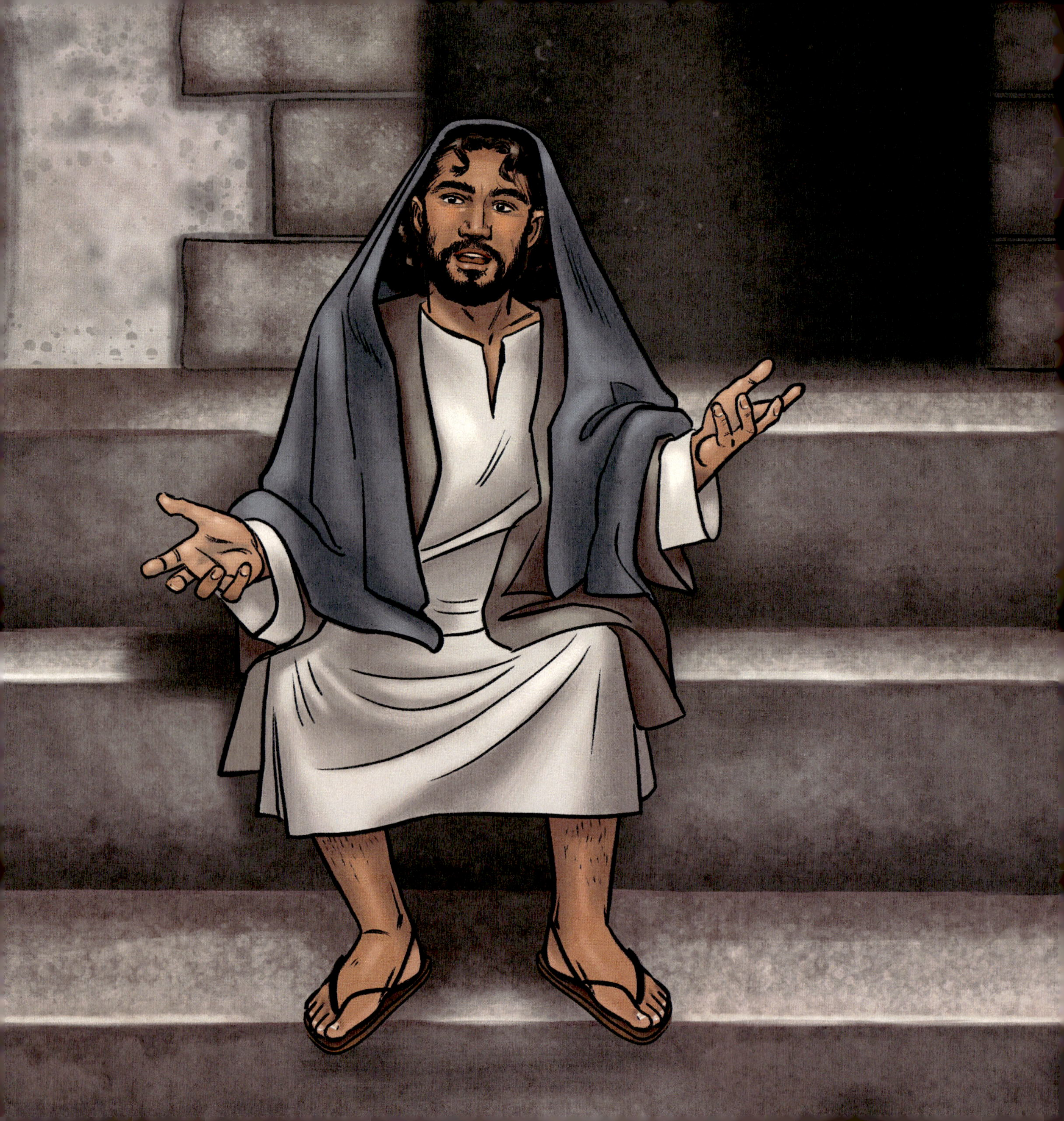

Mark's Gospel
STUDY #34

Jesus' Authority: 2/5 "Rejection"

📖 **Read:** Mark 12:1-12 (Section is from Mark 11:15 - 12:44)

💬 **Talk:**

1. In this passage, Jesus taught another parable in the temple. Remember that in this week leading up to Passover celebration, Jesus' authority is revealed.

2. Do you know what "consequences" are? *[a consequence is the result of an action]* What are some examples? *[throw a ball and it falls to the ground/break a law and receive punishment/softly answer an angry person to calm them down]* Jesus teaches that rejecting Him has very serious consequences. Do you think the Pharisees and chief priests were listening while He taught this? (v12)

3. In this parable a man builds a vineyard and hires people to take care of it. As the owner sent servants to the vineyard, were they treated better each time or worse? *[worse]* What happened to the man's son? *[the tenants of the field killed him]* What happened to the tenants after that? (v9) *[He destroys them and hires other tenants to care for the vineyard]*

4. Notice: This parable explains God's perspective on how Israel treated the prophets and His Word. When God sent prophets to Israel throughout the Old Testament, were they treated well, or increasingly worse? (see Hebrews 11) *[worse]* What happened to Jesus, God's own Son, when He came to earth? *[they killed Him]*

5. Read Psalm 118:22-23. Have you ever built a house or fort while playing outside? Did you ever hold a stick or brick and think, "Nah, this piece is too small" and then toss it away? You rejected it. This is what the religious leaders in the temple did to Jesus. They rejected Him. But what happens to the stone the builders reject? *[it becomes the most important stone in the building - the cornerstone (Ephesians 2:20)]*

6. How is Jesus the cornerstone of our salvation, the gospel, and the church? *[Jesus died to conquer sin and death, satisfy God's wrath, and fix our broken relationship with God. God's entire rescue plan of salvation rests on Jesus]*

❤️ **Pray:** God, there are many people in the world that reject Jesus. They want no other god but themselves. We pray for them - that their spiritual eyes would be opened and that they would turn from sin and become disciples of Jesus too. Help us live today in a way that honors Jesus as the chief Cornerstone.

🎵 **Sing:** "Crown Him With Many Crowns". (pg 101)   Also, "Come Behold the Wondrous Mystery" (not included in hymn section).

> **BEING JESUS' DISCIPLE MAY MEAN REJECTION BY PEOPLE**

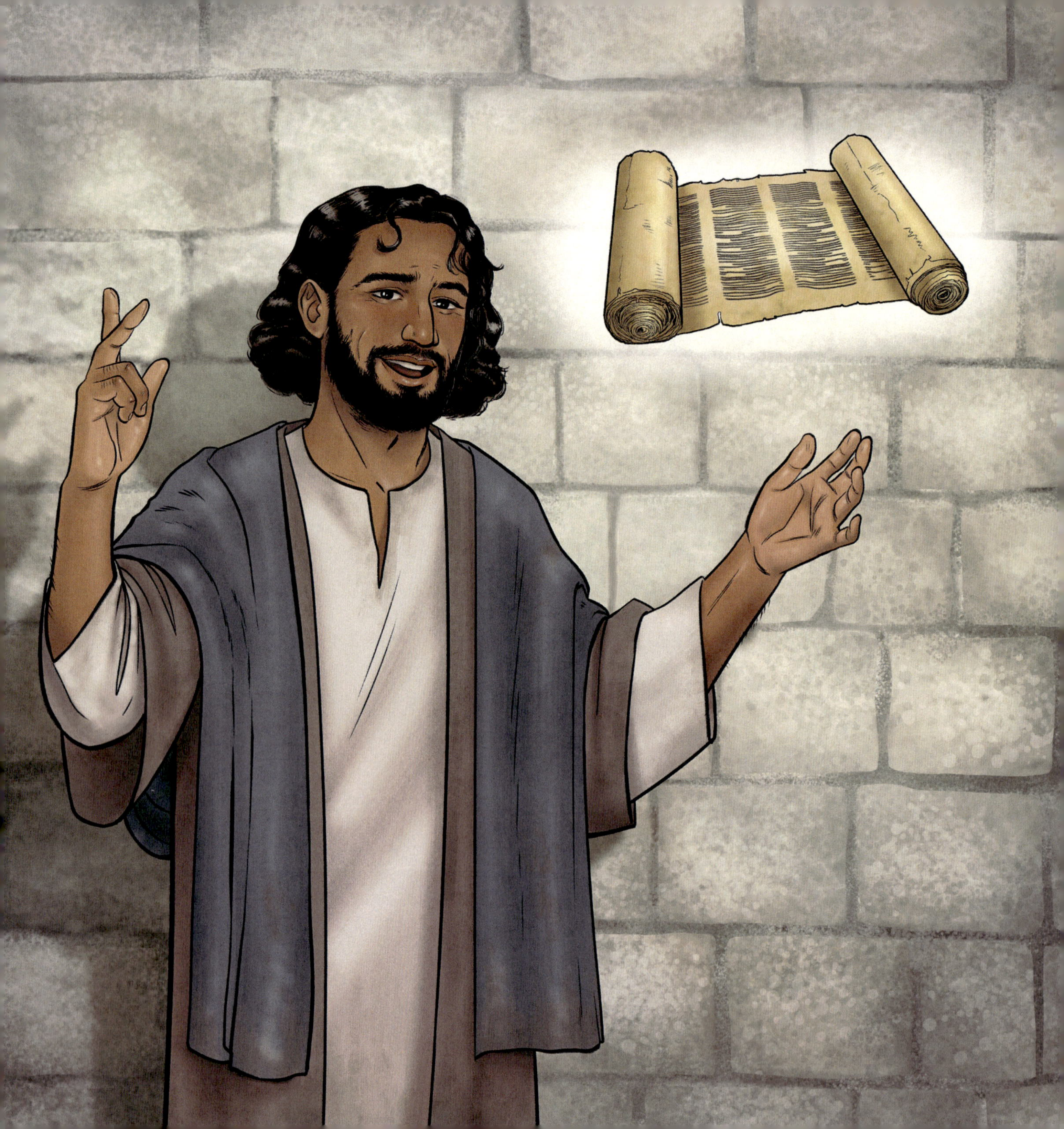

Mark's Gospel
STUDY #35

Jesus' Authority: 3/5 "Taxes & Eternity"

📖 **Read:** Mark 12:13-27 (Section is from Mark 11:15 - 12:44)

💬 **Talk:**

1. Jesus is teaching in the temple. Remember that in this week leading up to Passover celebration, Jesus is revealing His authority as He teaches.

2. The Pharisees attempt to trick Jesus into saying something that will either a) put Him out of favor with the people, "Yes, pay taxes to the oppressive Roman government, or b) make Him a rebel against Rome, "No, don't pay taxes to Rome." However, what does Jesus say in v17? *[give the money due to Caesar, since his face is on the coin; give to God the worship due to Him, since He is the Creator]* How did the Pharisees react? *[marveled]*

3. Though Jesus has authority over Caesar and Rome, He taught His disciples to honor governments that ruled over them. In the next section (vs18-27), we see how a disciple of Jesus interprets the Scriptures and teaches about God's power in eternity.

4. Do you know who the Sadducees were? *[small group of aristocratic, religious upper-class who cooperated with Roman rule]* The Sadducees interpreted the Old Testament differently than the Pharisees. (see "Extra Time" below)

5. To explain, the Old Testament Law said that if a man died, his unmarried younger brother should marry his wife. The scenario the Sadducees come up with (7 brothers all dying after each one married the woman) was not likely to ever happen. But Jesus doesn't address that. Instead, He teaches them.

- After the resurrection, when God's people enjoy His presence forever, will married people still be married? (v25) *[no]* Does Jesus talk about the resurrection like it's a real, future event? *[yes]*

6. By His answer, Jesus not only avoids their trap, but corrects their error in theology (teaching and beliefs) about the Bible. How does v27 end? *["you are badly mistaken!"]* Jesus is pointing everyone to what God intended in the scriptures, not what the scribes interpreted.

❤️ **Pray:** Father in Heaven, You have the authority to teach us what to believe and how to live. Earthly rulers often oppress and abuse. But You, Creator God, are different. You own us completely and call for complete submission yet give us eternal life! Help us be humble and accept the authority of Your Word.

🎵 **Sing:** "All Creatures of Our God and King". (pg 95)   Also, "Behold Our God" (not included in hymn section).

⇾ EXTRA TIME? ⇽

Read Acts 23:6-10. Talk about the differences between Pharisees and Sadducees given in this passage. Paul used this difference to stop an unjust trial. Now consider the two topics in today's study that Jesus explained to the Sadducees: the resurrection of the dead and the existence of angels (Mark 12:25) are real!

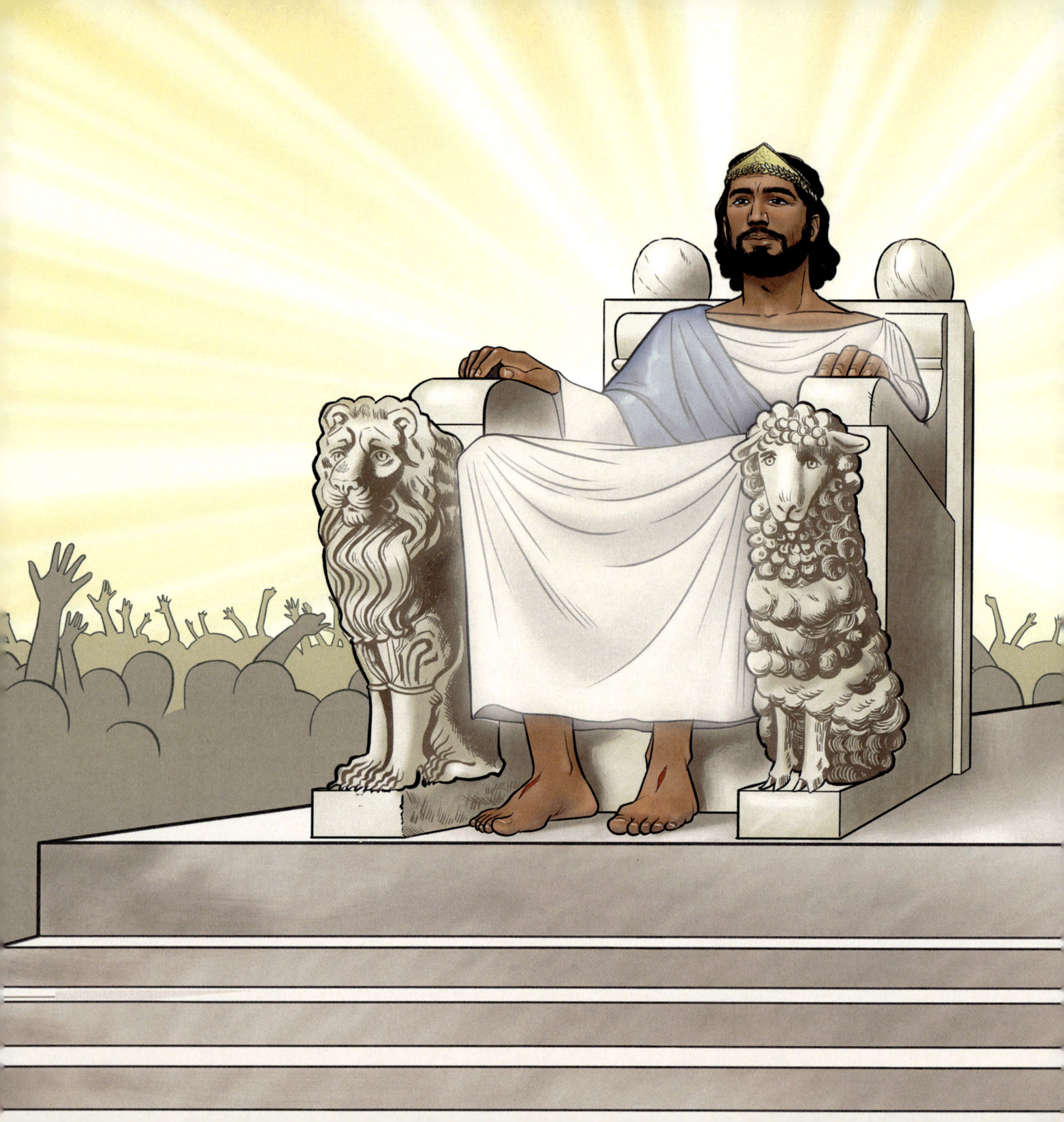

Mark's Gospel
STUDY #36

Jesus' Authority: 4/5 "Greatest Command"

📖 **Read:** Mark 12:28-37 (Section is from Mark 11:15 - 12:44)

💬 **Talk:**

1. Jesus is teaching in the temple; remember that in this week leading up to Passover celebration, Jesus is revealing His authority as He teaches.

2. Imagine you and a friend are looking for a lost ball. As you stand near some bushes, your friend says, "Oh, it's right in front of you!" You can't see it, and say, "Where?" Friend: "Right there!" You still don't see it, so you step to one side and suddenly you see it! The branches and leaves were blocking your view. Sometimes we need to view things differently to see clearly.

3. Does the scribe in vs28-34 act like someone competing with Jesus' popularity like the Pharisees? *[no]* What was the man's question? *[which command from God is the most important?]* Did you notice that Jesus' answer and the scribe's reply are basically the same? But what does the scribe add to what Jesus said? (v33) *[that loving God and your neighbor are more important than burnt offerings and sacrifices]* In other words, **religious activity means very little if your heart is not loving toward God or others.**

4. Next, Jesus taught that Messiah will be much more than a politician or king in the royal line of King David, He will be exalted to the right hand of God. (vs35-37)

- Psalm 110:1 can be a bit confusing, which is why Jesus asked the people a question about it. King David wrote in the Psalm, "The Lord (Yahweh) said to my Lord (Adonai), 'Sit at My right hand...'" Jesus then asks, "If the Messiah is a descendant of David, why would David call Him 'Lord'?"

- The scribes correctly believe that Messiah will be David's descendant. But their perspective is blocked, so Jesus points out their misunderstanding.

- **Truth: The Messiah is more than a political king in David's royal line - Jesus rules over the Kingdom of God the Father.**

❤️ **Pray:** God, we read today that the crowd gladly heard Jesus' teaching, and so do we. But, Father, help us take the truth of Your Word from our heads down to our hearts. Then we will worship You out of a heart of love for You and love for others.

🎵 **Sing:** "Jesus Shall Reign". (pg 106)   Also, "O Great God" (not included in hymn section).

⇉ EXTRA TIME? ⇇

The scribe in today's study correctly answered Jesus that God is most interested in our hearts, not in our religious activities. (verses 32-33) What do these verses say about this theme? 1 Samuel 15:22, Hosea 6:6, & Psalm 51:16-17

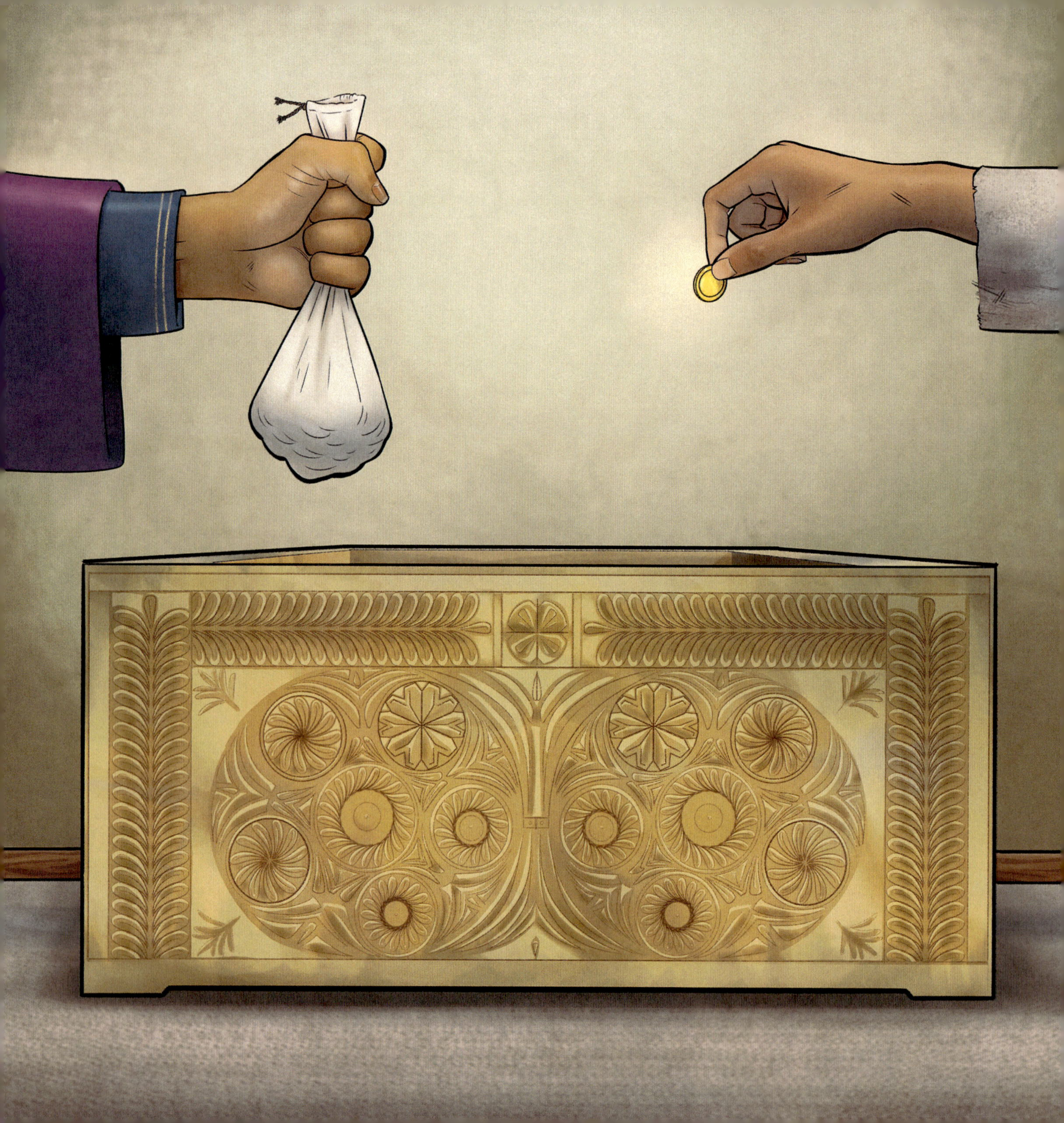

Mark's Gospel
STUDY #37

Jesus' Authority: 5/5 "Revealing the Heart"

📖 **Read:** Mark 12:38-44 (Section is from Mark 11:15 - 12:44)

💬 **Talk:**

1. Jesus is teaching in the temple; remember that in this week leading up to Passover celebration, Jesus is revealing His authority as He teaches.

2. The study today contrasts the scribes and religious leaders in Israel with a widow Jesus noticed at the temple. Let's work through the contrast to make it very clear.

3. Contrast the religious leaders and the widow:
   - Which one cared about appearing generous more than God's opinion of their heart? *[scribes]*
   - Which one expected the seats of honor at feasts? *[scribes]*
   - Which thought God deserved the best from them, rather than expecting the best in this life? *[the widow]*
   - Which one appeared to depend upon God to take care of them? *[maybe both did, but the widow was completely dependent on God with no other money]*

4. Some people believe that these verses teach us to give everything we own to God and live very poor and dependent on God. But this was not Jesus' point. **Jesus taught His disciples (and us too!) that our actions reveal our hearts.**

5. How did the actions of the scribes and rich people reveal their hearts? *[answers vary]* How did the actions of the widow reveal her heart? *[she trusted God the Father to care for her and was faithful to support the temple worship - she cared more about God's opinion than people's opinion]*

6. Think about your actions at church or in your home. Do you obey your parents or God so that people will think you a good person? Or do you serve God out of a heart of love for Him? **A true disciple of Jesus trusts God whether he or she has a lot or a little.**

❤️ **Pray:** Father, You see the heart and people only see the outside actions we do. It is hard to remember to daily live for You (Whom we have yet to see face to face) and not to live for other people's approval (whom we see every day). As we live each day, help us live as though You are the only one watching. Keep us from spiritual pride!

🎵 **Sing:** "The King of Love My Shepherd Is" (pg 109)

⇒ BEING JESUS' DISCIPLE MEANS CONTENTMENT ⇐
Contentment: realizing that God has given you everything you need for your present happiness.

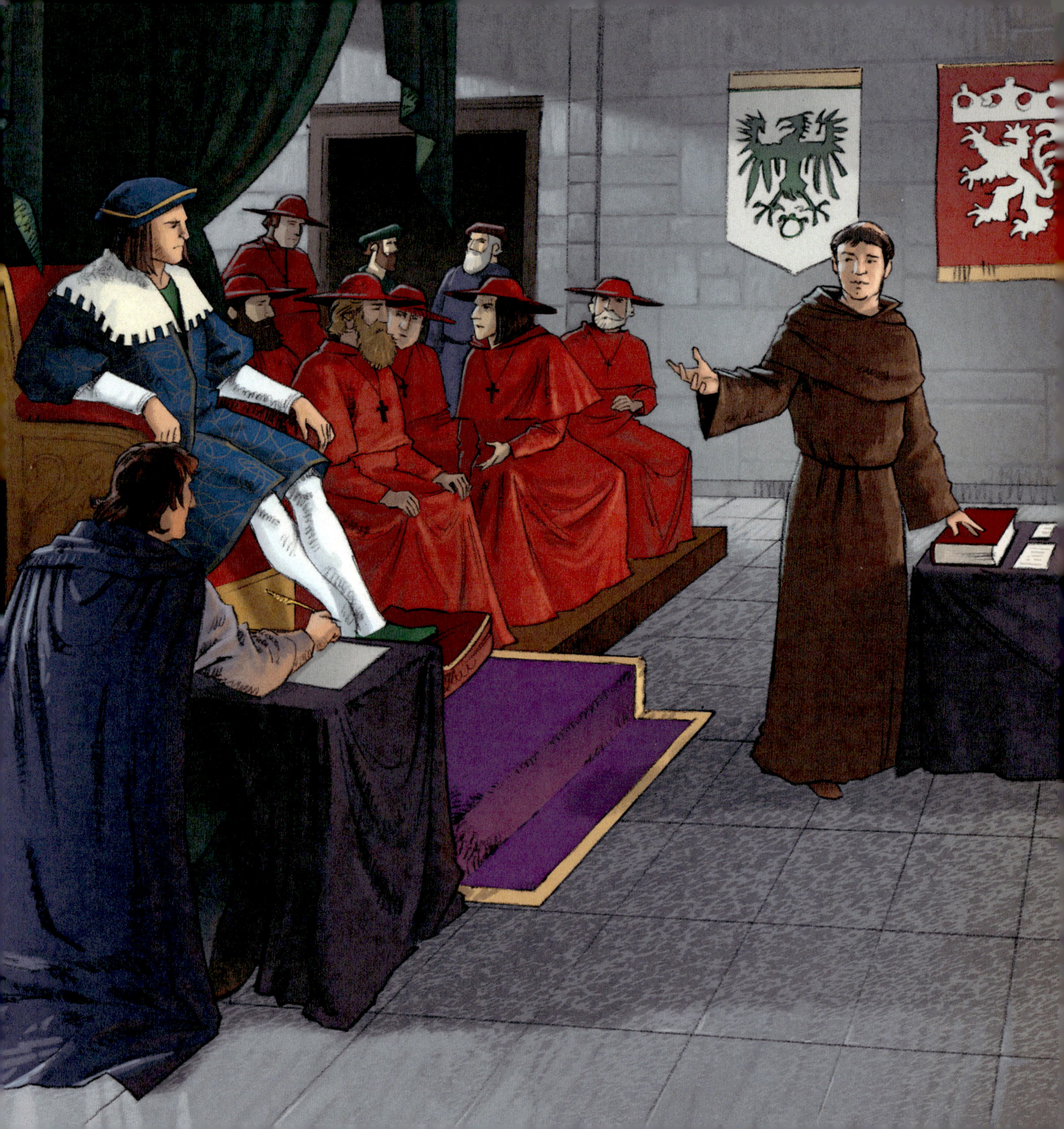

Mark's Gospel

STUDY #38

Signs of the End Times

Read: Mark 13:1-23

Talk:

1. Across from the Temple outside Jerusalem is the Mount of Olives. (maybe take a moment to look up a picture of Jerusalem from this hill) In this private setting on the Mount of Olives, Jesus teaches His disciples about the end times.
2. Here is an important principle with prophecy in the Bible. In several places in Scripture, when a prophet like Isaiah was instructed by the Holy Spirit to tell about the future, there was a NEAR and FAR fulfillment of the prophecy. Part of the prophecy would happen soon, while another part would happen centuries later. The trouble with understanding a prophecy is that no one knew when any part would take place. With this NEAR and FAR idea in mind, consider today's passage.
   - We can see in history that much of vs1-13 was fulfilled in the 1st century, soon after Jesus left the earth. Christians had to flee Judea in 67 AD due to persecution, and Rome completely destroyed the Jerusalem temple three years later. Vs1-13 was partially fulfilled NEAR to the time Jesus spoke these words.
   - We can see in history that much of vs14-23 has **not yet** happened. This has turned out to be FAR from the time Jesus spoke these words, at least by human measurement of time.
   - In either case, whether this prophecy is fulfilled NEAR or FAR, Jesus said in v7, "Do not be alarmed." As believers and disciples of Jesus, He wants us to be **aware** but not **alarmed**.
3. In a world of wars, illness, natural disasters and persecution, it would be easy to become afraid. But none of these things are out of God's control. None of these things are a surprise to Him. Our role as disciples is to obey God today and trust Him for tomorrow, enduring to the end.

Pray: Heavenly Father, You are in solid control of today and tomorrow. You are providentially moving all of history to the point where "every knee will bow and every tongue confess that Jesus Christ is Lord" for Your own glory, which You well deserve. We trust You to care for us today and we trust You for our eternity.

Sing: "This Is My Father's World". (pg 110) Also, "O Great God" (not included in hymn section).

EXTRA TIME?

The visual for this study is a rendering of Martin Luther standing before the Diet of Worms in 1521. Martin Luther was on trial for teaching doctrine that did not agree with the official Roman Catholic church. In truth, Luther's teaching was indeed more biblical. In light of Mark 13:9, Jesus knew that His disciples would be persecuted for following closely to Him.

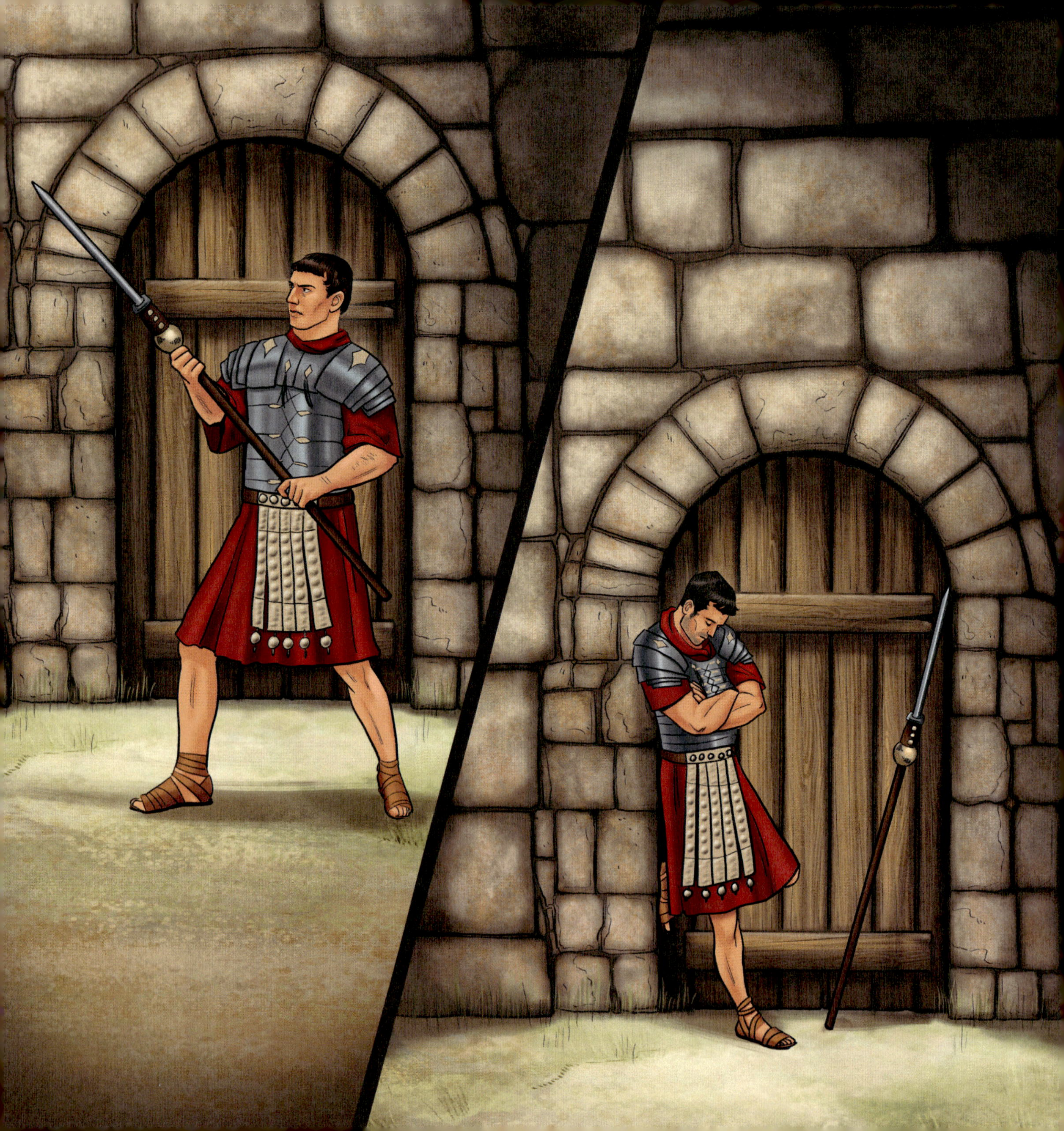

Mark's Gospel
STUDY #39

Be Vigilant

📖 **Read:** Mark 13:24-37

💬 **Talk:** Be Vigilant!

1. This is Jesus' message to His disciples. Jesus, the Son of Man and Son of God, will one day return. We do not know when exactly that will be, so what does Jesus command in v37? *[stay awake!]*

2. Two guards are watching a gate. Describe what you see in the picture for this study. What words would you use to describe the two guards? Would both guards be ready if someone tried to get past them? *[answers will vary; only one guard is ready]*

3. In vs24-27, what will the world's circumstances be like when Jesus returns one day? *[sun darkened, creation failing, etc]* Who will be rescued from these terrible circumstances? *[the "elect", believers]*

4. In vs28-31, what picture does Jesus use to illustrate His return? *[fig tree]* What are the first signs of spring or rainy season where you live? *[answers vary by geography]* When you see those signs, you know the season is changing. In the same way, when believers see the signs Jesus spoke of, then His return is soon.

- Note: this section can be very difficult to interpret. There are several ways of understanding the passage, but the next section tells us what to DO.

5. In vs32-37, how many times does "keep awake" or "stay awake" occur? *[4 times]*

6. Does Jesus command the disciples to figure out the exact time that He will return? *[no]* Does Jesus command us to try to figure out if our current circumstances exactly fit the signs He described? *[no]* What does Jesus command His disciples to do? *[stay awake!]*

7. As Jesus' disciple, be as vigilant as a guard on duty. When Jesus returns, don't be found distracted by life's cares or absentminded. Stay awake and minister to the people around you in the way God has called you to do. Jesus will return at just the right time: in God's time. Your job is to live like He might return today!

❤️ **Pray:** Father, we are excited for the day that Jesus returns. We long for the day when all the evil of the world is done away. Until the day we see Jesus face to face, help us to know You and follow Your Word.

🎵 **Sing:** "Amazing Grace" (pg 96)

⇉ EXTRA TIME? ⇇

Another way the Bible teaches us about staying "awake" and "vigilant" is when Paul instructs the reader to "See then that you walk circumspectly, not as fools but as wise" (Ephesians 5:15). In today's world, how do we 'stay awake' and walk wisely? *[avoid worldly thinking/lies, bad attitudes, careful choice of friends, daily choices]*

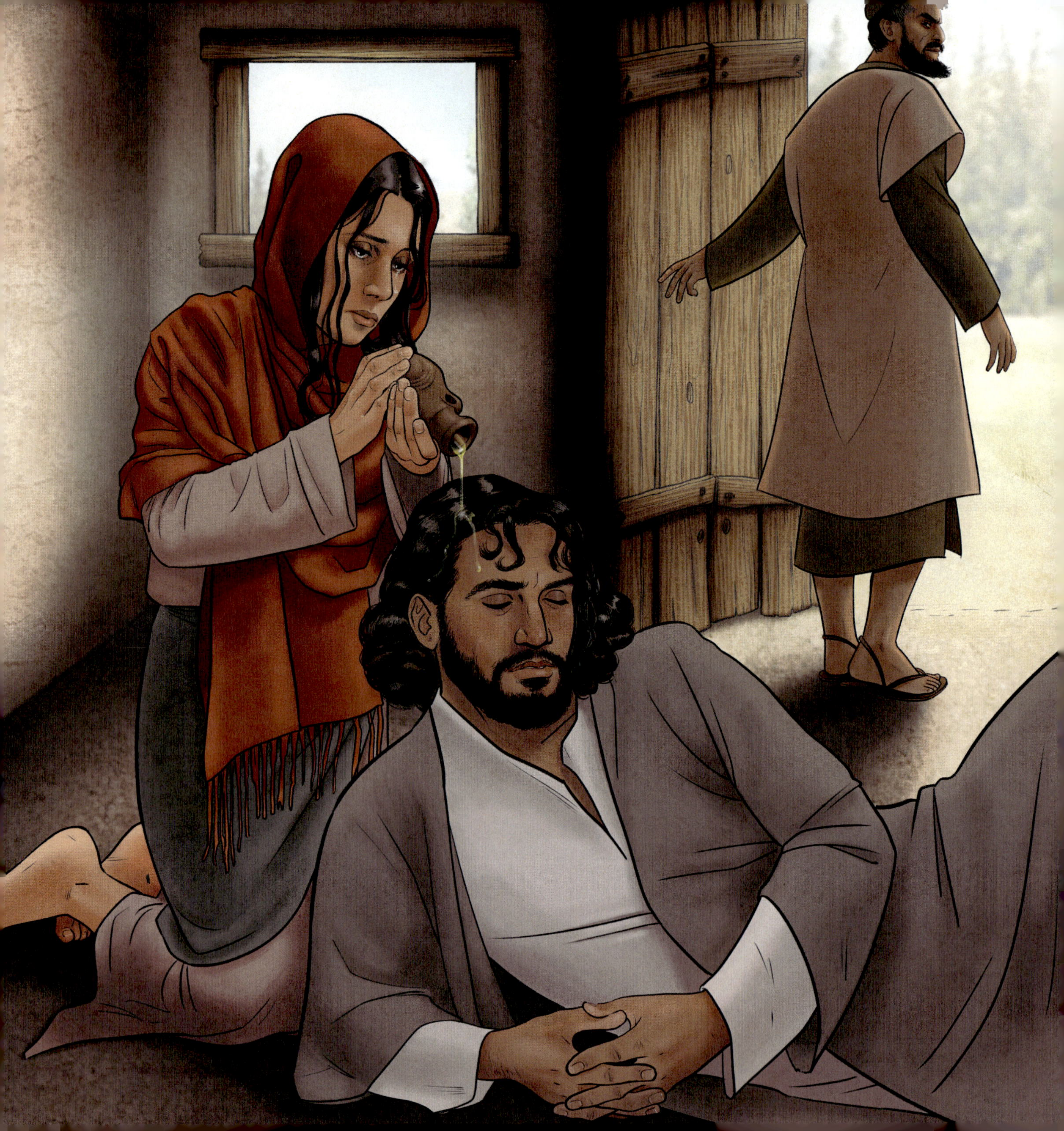

Mark's Gospel
STUDY #40

Anointed Lamb

📖 **Read:** Mark 14:1-11

💬 **Talk:**

1. The passage today tells us that the religious leaders were again looking for a reason to accuse Jesus. But how far did their anger and jealousy drive them? What were they looking to do to Jesus? (v1) *[kill Jesus]* But what did they fear? *[the crowd that was always with Jesus. Jesus was popular with the common people]* Do you see why Jesus was eventually arrested late on a holiday night? *[yes, no crowd to 'defend' Jesus]*

2. In your own words, describe the events of vs3-9 in the home of Simon the leper. Take a minute to talk among yourselves about what occurred.

3. In v8, it is possible that the woman believed she was anointing Jesus to be king, as other kings of Israel in the Old Testament. (as in 1 Samuel 16:11-13) If so, Jesus corrects this by declaring that the anointing of His head with oil was actually for what? (v8) *[for His burial, not ascending to a throne]* During this week leading up to the crucifixion, does anyone else do a beautiful, good work to Jesus like this woman? *[no]*

4. In contrast, what is Judas looking to do? *[betray Jesus]* Jesus promises that the woman's kind act will never be forgotten (v9). But we must also notice: Will Judas' wicked act also be remembered wherever the gospel is preached? *[yes!]*

5. Sandwiched between two acts of extraordinary hate is this woman's act of extraordinary love and devotion. Similar to the widow in Mark 12:42, she did what she could for God. One woman could only give a little. One woman gave a lot. Both were faithful to God. Both were praised by Jesus.

❤️ **Pray:** God, You deserve our devotion. No act of sacrifice that we could make compares to the sacrifice Jesus made for us. May we be willing to offer you everything we are and own, even our lives, for Your service. Thank You for all You have done for us.

🎵 **Sing:** "All Creatures of Our God and King". (pg 95) Also, "Jesus, Thank You" (not included in hymn section).

⇒ EXTRA TIME? ⇐

Read Matthew 26:6-13 and John 12:1-8. Who is the woman that anointed Jesus with the expensive oil? *[Mary, sister to Martha and Lazarus. They lived in Bethany, not far from Jerusalem]*

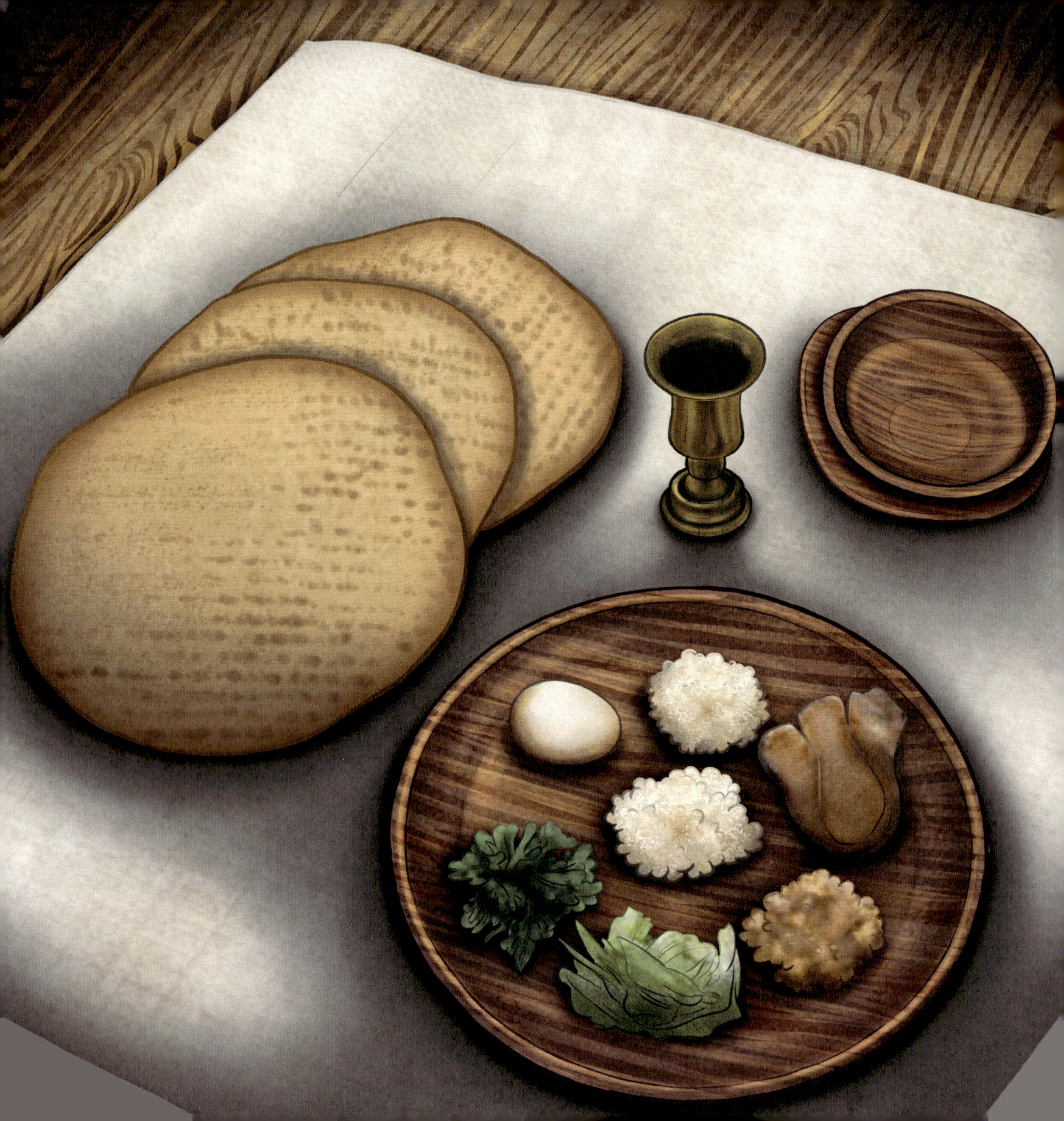

Mark's Gospel
STUDY #41

The Last Passover Lamb

📖 **Read:** Mark 14:12-31 *see "Extra Time" below

💬 **Talk:** Jesus knew what God the Father had planned for Him.

1. The Son of God came to earth to rescue sinners. Jesus **had** to give His life to rescue many. Not only did He know generally that He would be put to death, He knew specific details about how the next day would unfold. What details did Jesus give to the disciples in vs13-15? *[specific man carrying water, specifics about the conversation they would have, specific house, specific room]*

2. In that culture, people did not sit at tables using chairs. In the 1st century, the Jewish people would recline on their left side, propped up on their elbow and eating with their right hand.

3. **The Betrayer**: Judas sat close to Jesus at this last supper: 1) It gave Judas a final chance to repent, but he did not. 2) The close fellowship at this meal highlights the depth of betrayal by Judas (Psalm 41:9) Does Jesus seem angry or sad about betrayal? *[sad]*

4. **The New Covenant**: Jesus gives the disciples something new to replace the old covenant under Moses and the law. What are the two elements from the Lord's Supper (Communion) that help us remember this new covenant? *[bread and the cup]* What are these to remind us of? *[Jesus body and blood - His sacrifice]* **After Jesus' resurrection, the disciples realize that Jesus was the last Passover lamb!**

5. **The Prediction**: After they sang a hymn together (likely a Psalm to close the Passover meal), Jesus leads the disciples out of Jerusalem to the Mount of Olives. Jesus tells them that when He is arrested, all of them will run away from Him, at least initially. Which of the disciples is confident that would never happen? *[Peter]*

6. When James and John asked for special privileges (10:37), the other disciples were unhappy with them (10:41). But when Peter assures Jesus of His loyalty, how do the other disciples respond? (v31) *[they all agree]*

❤️ **Pray:** God, we remember Jesus and His sacrifice. Every time our church gathers to celebrate communion together we remember how Jesus, the perfect Son of God, gave Himself to rescue us from the judgment we all deserve. Thank You, Jesus, for enduring the cross and the shame of it all. We gratefully remember.

🎵 **Sing:** "The King of Love My Shepherd Is" (pg 109) or a song your family knows that is based on a Psalm.

⇉ EXTRA TIME? ⇇
As you read the passage for today, consider reclining on the floor as they did in the 1st century. Reference the visual for this study as well as paragraph #2. Maybe a pillow or blanket could substitute as the table around which the disciples gathered.

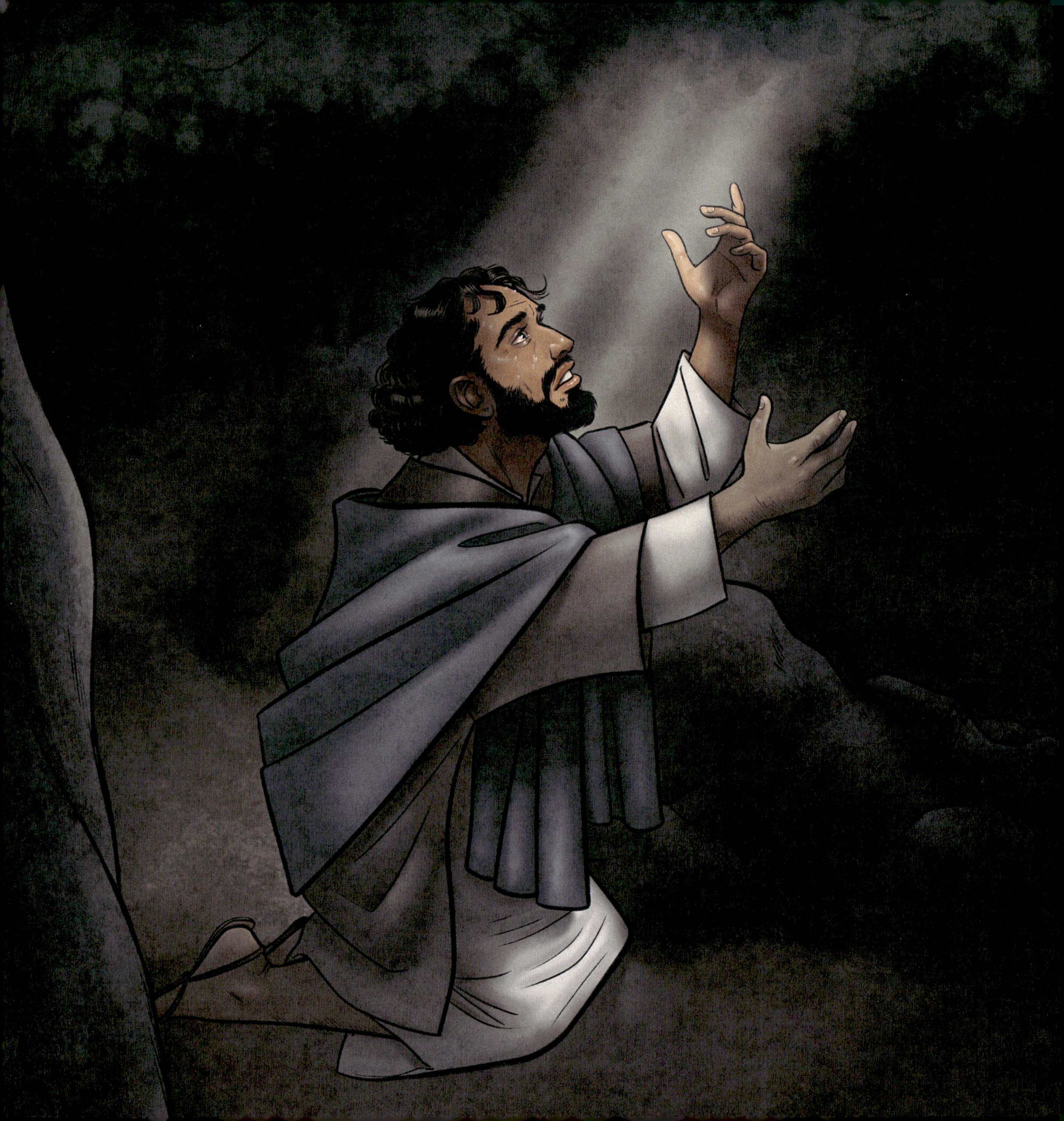

Mark's Gospel
STUDY #42

Prayer & Betrayal in Gethsemane

📖 **Read:** Mark 14:32-52

💬 **Talk:**

1. Jesus told His disciples to stay awake. Staying up late was a normal part of Passover celebration, remembering Moses' long-ago instruction that the Israelites stay up so their departure from Egypt would not be delayed.

2. **Watching**: When Jesus went to the Garden of Gethsemane after the Passover meal, He told eight disciples to stay in one place (maybe the garden entrance?) and to watch - to keep a look out. Who did Jesus take further into the garden? *[Peter, James and John]*

   - What is the reason they were to "watch and pray" in v38? *[that they not fall to temptation]* What was Jesus doing while they were sleeping? *[praying to God about the suffering about to happen on the cross]*

   - When Jesus told the disciples to "watch", He knew Judas and the Jewish leaders would arrest Him. He knew the disciples were sleepy and warned them to prepare themselves for the trials of that night with prayer.

3. **Praying**: In v37, why do you think Jesus asked this question to Peter, specifically? For help, read v29. *[Jesus asked Peter this question because Peter confidently said he would never run from Jesus to save his own life]*

   - In the garden, Jesus prayed in preparation for the most difficult trial anyone would ever face. What was the trial? *[dying for the sins of the world]* The disciples would also be facing a trial. What was it? *[answers vary: temptation to run away when Jesus was arrested; fear upon Jesus' death; confusion at resurrection, etc.]*

   - Jesus prepared for His very great trial by praying to His Father for strength. He obediently followed what God wanted Him to do. Did the disciples prepare? *[no]* Did they courageously stand with Jesus when He was arrested? (v50) *[no, they ran away]*

❤️ **Pray:** Father, our strength to endure hard things doesn't come from us, it comes from walking through life very closely to You! Help us in the trials we face today and in the future. We confess our weakness to endure trials and stay faithful like Jesus. Thank You for Your mercy toward us even when we do fail.

🎵 **Sing:** "God Moves in a Mysterious Way". (pg 103) Also, "His Mercy is More" (not included in hymn section).

⇉ **BEING JESUS' DISCIPLE MEANS GROWING THROUGH FAILURE** ⇇

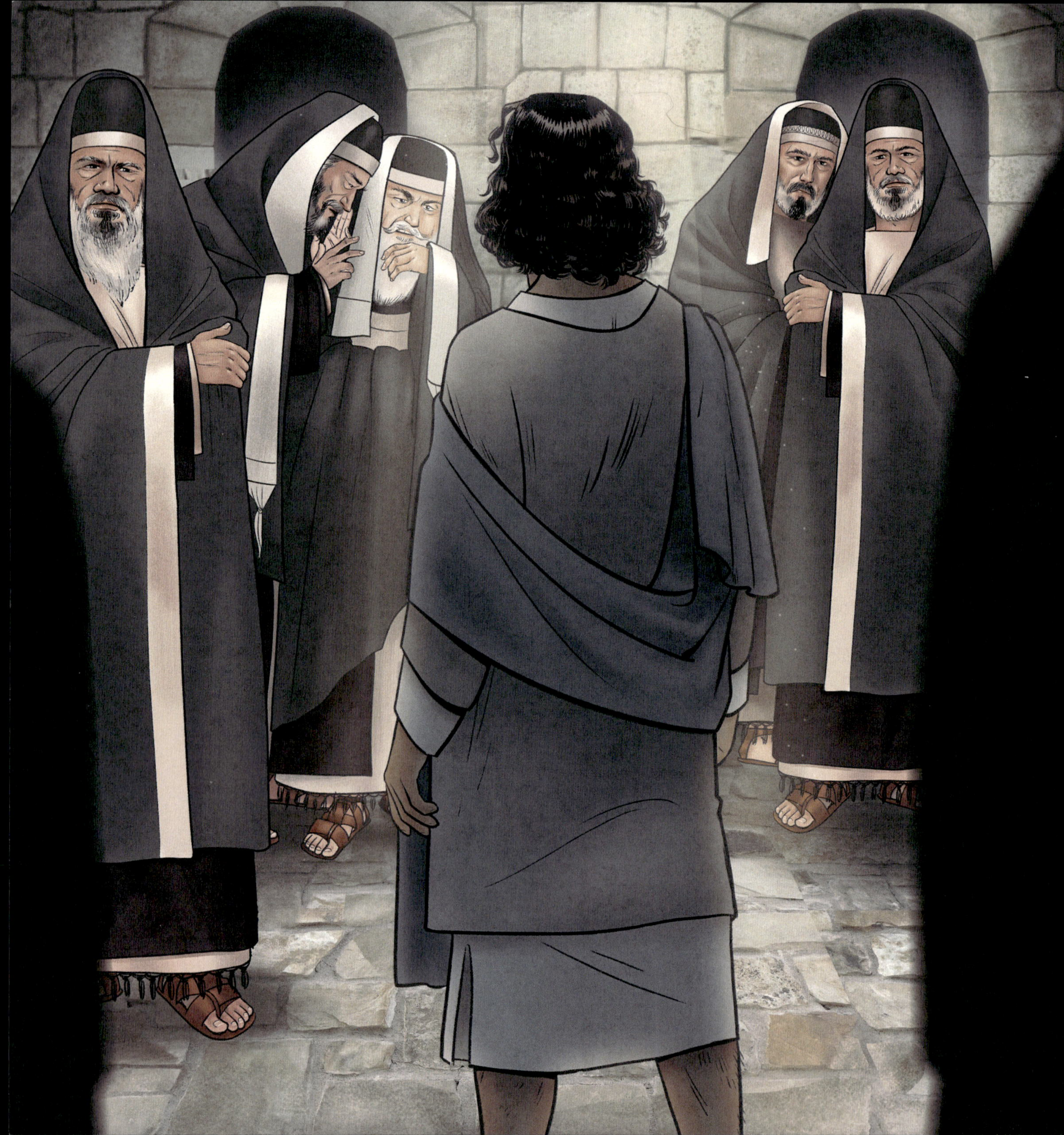

Mark's Gospel
STUDY #43

The Jewish Trial

📖 **Read:** Mark 14:53-72

💬 **Talk:**

1. As Jesus was taken to the chief priests for a trial, who followed behind Jesus and the soldiers? *[Peter]* Do you think Peter and the other disciples feared for their lives? *[yes]*

2. For hours the religious leaders heard false testimony from people who twisted Jesus' words and change what He taught, trying to convict Him to a death sentence. But what was their problem? (v59) *[their accusations and facts did not agree]*

   - Because they cannot successfully lie about Jesus, the high priest begins to question Jesus himself. When Jesus answers in v62, He quotes Psalm 110:1 and Daniel 7:13-14. Was the high priest pleased with this answer? *[no, he became very angry]*

   - The high priest accused Jesus of blasphemy, meaning that Jesus made Himself equal with God. But did Jesus really blaspheme God? *[no, because He really is God, the Messiah!]*

3. Where is Peter during this unfair trial? *[outside in the courtyard]* What was the weather like? *[cold/cool]*

4. How many times did Peter deny that he knew Jesus? *[three times]* How did Peter respond when he realized and remembered what Jesus had told him the night before? *[he wept]*

5. Think back on the last several studies. We know several things about Peter that led to his spiritual failure at this time. Do you see any of these in your life?

   - Over-confidence - Peter was so sure of his loyalty to Jesus.
   - Gripping fear - all the disciples were struggling between fear & faith.
   - Absent prayer - Jesus had challenged them to pray. They didn't.
   - Unbelief - Jesus warned Peter several times and Peter did not take it seriously.

❤️ **Pray:** Father, You know our every weakness. Even before we face temptation, You know what we need to remain faithful to You. Jesus is a perfect example for us: of love for God and others, of faithful submission to Your will, and kindness for those who crucified Him. May Your Word and Spirit grow the character of Jesus in us!

🎵 **Sing:** "Fairest Lord Jesus". (pg 102)   Also, "Wonderful, Merciful Savior" (not included in hymn section).

⇘ **EXTRA TIME?** ⇙

Look up the two passages listed in paragraph #2 and notice the phrases that Jesus quoted to the high priest.

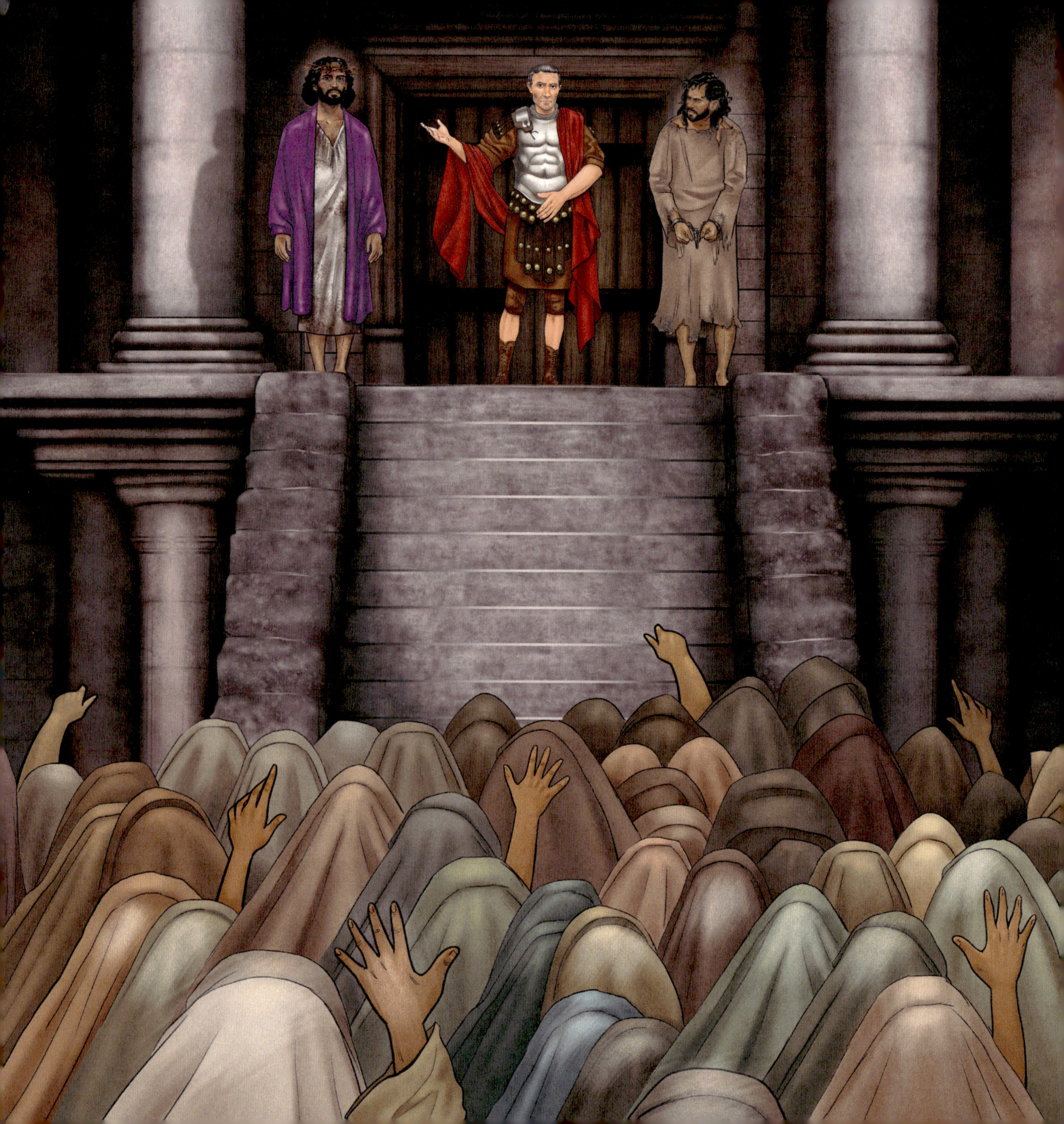

Mark's Gospel
STUDY #44
The Roman Trial

📖 **Read:** Mark 15:1-20

💬 **Talk:**

1. Study #43 looked at the Jewish trial of Jesus. In this study we will see how Jesus was treated by the Romans. Do you know why Jesus had to be taken to Pilate after the Jewish religious leaders judged Him? *[they needed Rome's permission to execute anyone]*

2. In vs4-5, what was Pilate's reaction to Jesus refusing to answer all of the made-up charges? *[amazed that Jesus did not defend Himself]* Jesus is practicing all he has preached. He is humbly serving and not defending Himself or making Himself great.

3. What clue does v10 give us that Pilate knew the accusations against Jesus were made up and false? *[Pilot knew the chief priests were jealous of Jesus]*

4. As Pilate felt the pressure from the crowd to condemn Jesus to death, v14 tells us that Pilate knew Jesus was innocent. What did Pilot ask the mob? *["Why, what evil has He done?"]*

5. In Rome, politics were important. If Pilate and Herod did not keep their region in good order, Caesar could remove them from power. Remember how Jesus entered Jerusalem to a cheering crowd? In vs13-15, does it seem like more political unrest would occur if Pilate did not order Jesus to be crucified? *[yes, it would have looked like Pilot lost control of the area]* So did Pilate condemn Jesus because a) Jesus broke the law, or b) because Pilate thought it would keep the peace? *[b) because Pilot was trying to keep peace in Jerusalem]*

6. How did the Roman guards mock Jesus? *[gave Him a purple robe like a king, gave Him crown of thorns like a king, kneel before Him and call Him "King of the Jews"]*

- To the soldiers, Jesus was just like any other Jewish peasant. Do you think they had any idea Who He really is?

❤️ **Pray:** Heavenly Father, Your Son was mocked, and scorned, and rejected by everyone. We know that all of Jesus' suffering had to happen this way, because it was Your will. His suffering and death show us just how much You hate sin - my sin. Thank You for sending Jesus to rescue us from our sin and take our punishment on Himself!

🎵 **Sing:** "O Worship the King" (pg 108)

⇾ **BEING JESUS' DISCIPLE MEANS TRUSTING GOD'S PLAN** ⇽

My God, my God, why a[rt thou]
forsaken me? why art thou so far
from helping me, and fro[m the wor]ds
of my roaring? O my God, I cry in the
day time, but thou hearest not; and in
the night season, and am not silent.
But thou art holy, O thou that
inhabitest the praises of Israel. Our
fathers trusted in thee: they trusted,
and thou didst deliver them.
They cried unto thee, and were
delivered: they trusted in thee, and
were not confounded. But I am a
worm, and no man; a reproach of
men, and despised of the people. All
they that see me laugh me to scorn:
they shoot out the lip, they shake the
head, saying, He trusted on the
LORD that he would deliver him: let
him deliver him, seeing he delighted
in him. But thou art he that took me
out of the womb: thou didst make me
hope when I was upon my mother's
breasts. I was cast upon thee from my
mother's belly. Be not far from me;
for trouble is near; for there is none to
help. Many bulls have compassed me:
strong bulls of Bashan have beset me
round. They gaped upon me with
their mouths, as a ravening and a
roaring lion. I am poured out like
water, and all my bones are out of
joint: my heart is like wax; it is melted
in the midst of my bowels. My
strength is dried up like a potsherd;
and my tongue cleaveth to my jaws;
and thou hast brought me into the
dust of death. For dogs have
compassed me: the assembly
wicked have inclosed m[e]
pierced my hands and m[y feet]
tell all my bones. They [look and stare]
upon me. They p[art my garments]
among them, a[nd cast lots upon my]
vesture. But b[e not thou far from me,]
O LORD
to help [me]

Mark's Gospel
— STUDY #45 —

God's Plan: the Crucifixion of Christ

📖 **Read:** Mark 15:21-39

💬 **Talk:**

1. **Jesus' death on the cross was part of God's rescue plan** for mankind ever since Genesis 3 when sin became part of life on earth.

2. **Jesus knew that His suffering and death was part of God's plan.** Look up these verses and read them out loud: Mark 8:31, 9:30-32, 10:32-34.

3. **Many of the themes from the Gospel of Mark are seen in this passage.** We see how Jesus really is King, even though mocked as a king. We see how He is becoming great by making Himself low, just as He had been teaching. We see how Jesus is serving others more than Himself by giving His life as a ransom for many (all people who believe God in faith).

4. Look up Galatians 4:4-5 together and read it out loud.

- What was the "fullness of time"? *[the right time in history / the point in time when Jesus should come to earth / the "stage was set"]*

- According to these verses, what was the purpose for Jesus becoming human like us? *[to redeem those who are under the law and to make us the children of God]*

5. **God's rescue plan for mankind was accomplished in the death of Jesus.** For every leader of every false religion in the world, their death is the end. But was death the end for Jesus? *[no!]* The resurrection of Jesus proves that Jesus was God. To those who trust in Jesus for salvation, God doesn't hold our sins against us for breaking His law. He forgives us. When Jesus rose again, He proved He had the power and the right to forgive us.

❤️ **Pray:** Heavenly Father, thank You for sending Jesus to earth. We could not rescue ourselves from the wrath of God. What a wonderful Savior Jesus is! He perfectly followed Your plan and obediently did Your will. Help us to tell others the good news that people can have a relationship with God.

🎵 **Sing:** "Amazing Grace". (pg 96)   Also, "Jesus, Thank You" (not included in hymn section).

⇞ EXTRA TIME? ⇟

God told the world many centuries before this how Messiah would come to earth and suffer. Can you find the verses in Mark 15 where these Old Testament prophecies are fulfilled in the death of Jesus Christ?
- Psalm 22:1 - [verse 34]   Psalm 22:6-8 - [verses 29-32]   Psalm 22:16-18 - [verses 24-25]
- Isaiah 53:3-6 - [verses 29-32, 36]   Isaiah 53:7, 12 - [verses 5, 27]

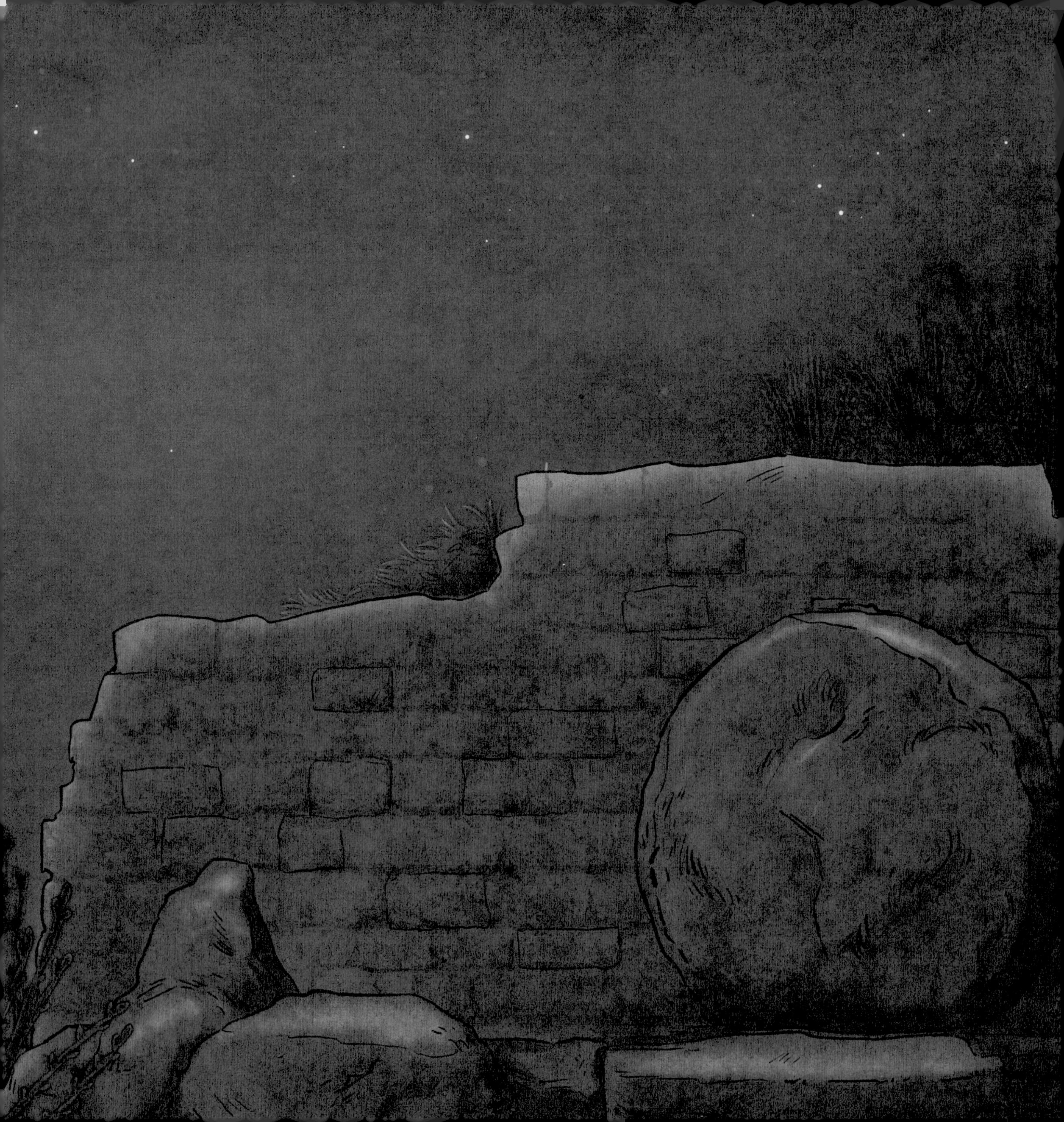

Mark's Gospel
STUDY #46

Being Jesus' Disciple

📖 **Read:** Mark 15:40-47

💬 **Talk:**

1. Do you remember Study #1? One of the main themes of the Gospel of Mark is "Being Jesus' Disciple"? Throughout this Gospel, Mark has described for us what it means to be Jesus' disciple. As we have read the book, were you ever surprised by the types of people who become disciples? This study is yet another surprise.

2. In the passage for this study, we discover that not all the religious leaders in Jerusalem believed that Jesus deserved death and shame. Who wanted to bury Jesus respectfully? *[Joseph of Arimathea]*

3. In the Roman empire, when a political criminal was executed, the body belonged to Rome. Permission to bury had to be obtained from a Roman official. To whom did Joseph go to ask for permission to bury Jesus' body? *[Pilate]*

4. Did you notice the phrase "took courage"? Why do you think Joseph needed to work up the courage to approach Pilate? *[If Joseph were connected to Jesus, then 1) Pilate might arrest Joseph too, thinking him a sympathizer, and 2) the rest of the Sanhedrin and religious leaders might remove Joseph from his position and power]* Joseph wasn't the only one afraid to be associated with Jesus at this time. Who else had run away the night before? *[all the disciples]*

5. It is a surprise that at the death of Jesus we find this man who had made up his mind that Jesus was Messiah. At the moment when no one wanted to be connected to Jesus, Joseph stepped out in courage to honor the Son of God by burying Him. Has following Jesus cost you anything?

6. What other unexpected and faithful people did you read about in vs40-41 and 47? *[it is surprising that the women, and not many disciples, were present throughout Jesus' death and burial]*

❤️ **Pray:** Father, whatever it may cost us to follow You, help us be faithful. Strengthen our trust and faith in You in the trials we will undoubtedly face. Being Jesus' disciple may cost us power, position, wealth, and popularity, but we do not want to be ashamed of the One Who has washed our guilt away. Thank You for Jesus.

🎵 **Sing:** "Come My Soul With Every Care". (pg 100)   Also, "All I Have is Christ" (not included in hymn section).

⇉ EXTRA TIME? ⇇
Jesus' burial is important to the gospel story - "Jesus was born, lived, died, was buried, and rose again." He lived a fully human life and died a fully human death. Because he went through our experience of death, we can be assured that he conquered death and that death cannot keep God's people either! What a hope we have in Christ!

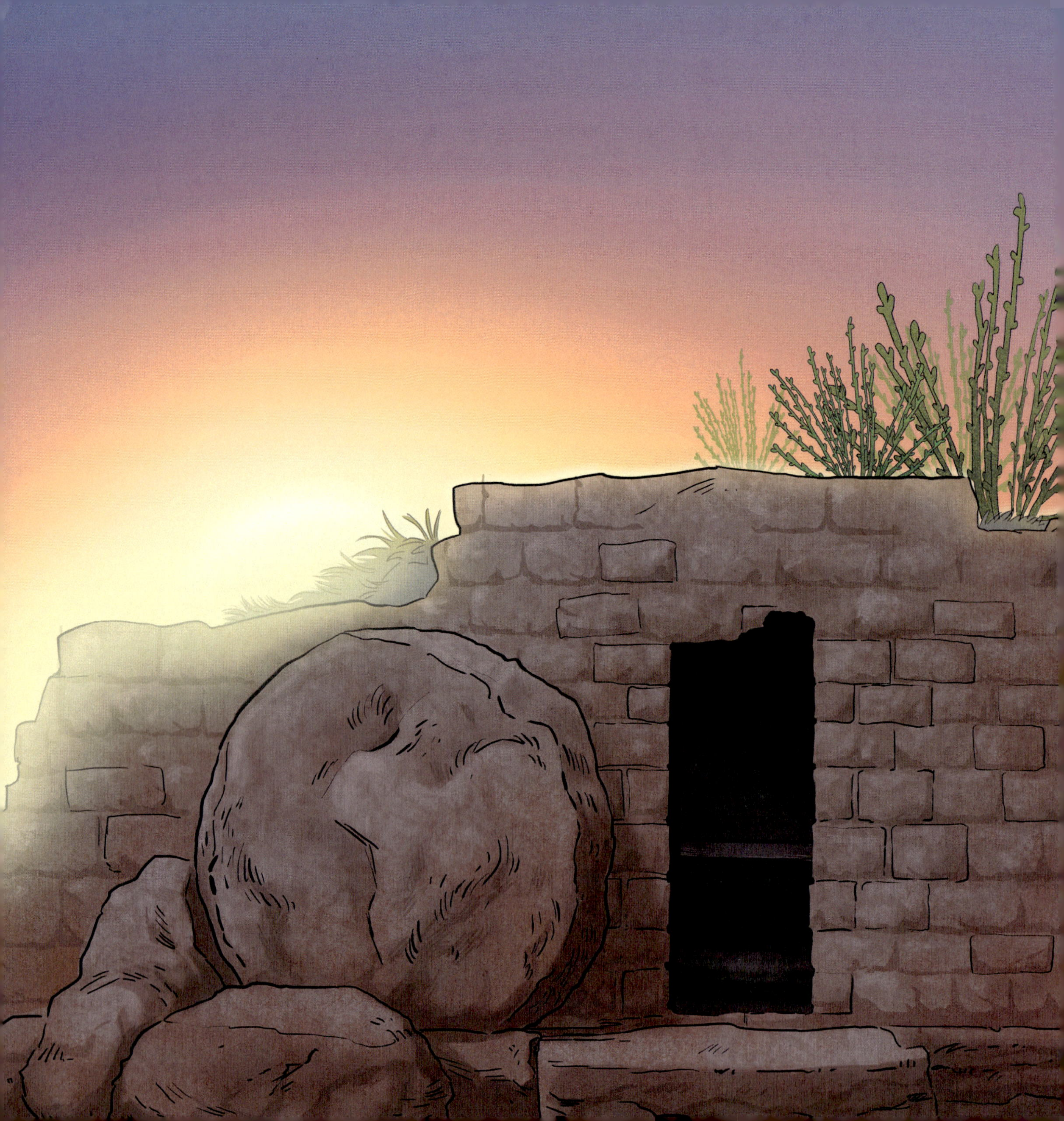

Mark's Gospel
— STUDY #47 —

Resurrection!

📖 **Read:** Mark 16

💬 **Talk:**

1. Throughout the gospels (Matthew, Mark, Luke, John), God included people from all walks of life in His kingdom. Salvation in Jesus was offered to everyone: Jews and Gentiles, rich and poor, famous and infamous, man and woman. Think of it... Shepherds attended His birth, and royalty from afar brought Him gifts. He ate with sinners and tax collectors, yet challenged the most brilliant minds in the temple. Anyone and everyone could hear the gospel.

2. What three women visited the tomb of Jesus, according to Mark? *[Mary Magdalene, another Mary, and Salome]*

3. Have you ever prepared to start a project or schoolwork, only to discover that you forgot the book at home? You felt like all the setup work was for nothing! You had to waste time to go home and get your book!

   - Now look at 16:3. The women were almost to the tomb when they remembered: "There's a huge stone in the way! How are we going to move that?" They traveled all the way to the tomb, only to remember that they could not get into the tomb! Just at that moment, they looked up and saw that the stone was already moved. What emotions do you think they felt in that moment? *[confusion, surprise, scared or angry that someone might have stolen the body]*

4. The fact that shepherds and women were given great privilege in the birth, death, and resurrection of Messiah, tells us something about God's love for *every soul*. The culture of their day marginalized certain kinds of people, and those were often the people that Jesus ministered to.

5. Your Savior is alive. The tomb in Jerusalem is still quite empty today. If you will confess, believe, and trust Jesus with your eternity, God promises forgiveness. If you are not yet a disciple of Jesus, the invitation to you is still open!

❤️ **Pray:** Father, in Your love You offer salvation to all of us. Thank You! What a joy to think that we serve a risen Savior Who is alive today. We look forward to the day Jesus returns, please let it be soon!

🎵 **Sing:** "Christ the Lord is Risen Today" to celebrate the resurrection of Jesus from the dead. (pg 98)   Also, "Behold Our God" (not included in hymn section).

⇉ **BEING JESUS' DISCIPLE MEANS BELIEVING** ⇇

If you believe Jesus is your sinless Savior, and that God raised Him from the dead, you will be saved. (Rom.10)

Family Harmony

Singing in your home, whatever quality it may have, communicates to the next generation that 1) this faith we speak of is real, and 2) it is real to the parents and adults in the room.

Joyful singing of gospel truth after each study helps connect scripture to the heart. The very best hymns and songs we can sing are those that bring Scripture to mind!

The songs in this collection are familiar to many and produced for you to use. There may be songs familiar to your family that come to mind during the course of the study, and choosing to sing that song may have great benefit too.

If a song in this collection is unfamiliar, consider reading the poetry aloud.

About that singing voice...

Someone once said, "Christian music is the intersection of truth and beauty." While you may not feel that your singing voice conveys beauty, children love to hear their parents / grandparents sing anyway.

Chords are included so the family guitar, ukulele or balalaika can be incorporated in worship.

All Creatures of Our God and King

*All Your works shall give thanks to You, O LORD,
and Your saints will bless You. Psalm 145:10*

1. All creatures of our God and King, lift up your voice and with us sing, Alleluia! Alleluia! Thou burning sun with golden beam, thou silver moon with softer gleam, O praise Him, O praise Him, Alleluia, alleluia, alleluia!

2. Thou rushing wind that art so strong, ye clouds that sail in heav'n along, O praise Him, alleluia! Thou rising morn, in praise rejoice, ye lights of evening find a voice, O praise Him, O praise Him, Alleluia, alleluia, alleluia!

3. And all ye men of tender heart, forgiving others, take your part, O sing ye, alleluia! Ye who long pain and sorrow bear, praise God, and on Him cast your care, O praise Him, O praise Him, Alleluia, alleluia, alleluia!

4. Let all things their Creator bless, and worship Him in humbleness, O praise Him, alleluia! Praise, praise the Father, praise the Son, and praise the Spirit, Three in One, O praise Him, O praise Him, Alleluia, alleluia, alleluia!

TEXT: Francis of Assisi, 1225; trans. William H. Draper, 1910
MUSIC: *Geistliche Kirchengesäng*, 1623, harm. R. Vaughan Williams, 1904

LASST UNS ERFREUEN
88.88.8 with alleluias

Amazing Grace

For by grace you have been saved through faith; and that not of yourselves, it is the gift of God; not as a result of works, so that no one may boast. Ephesians 2:8-9

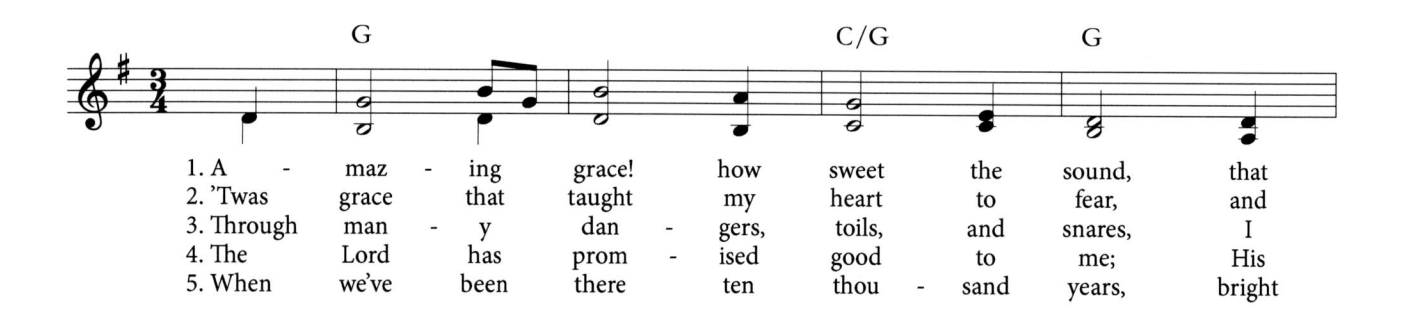

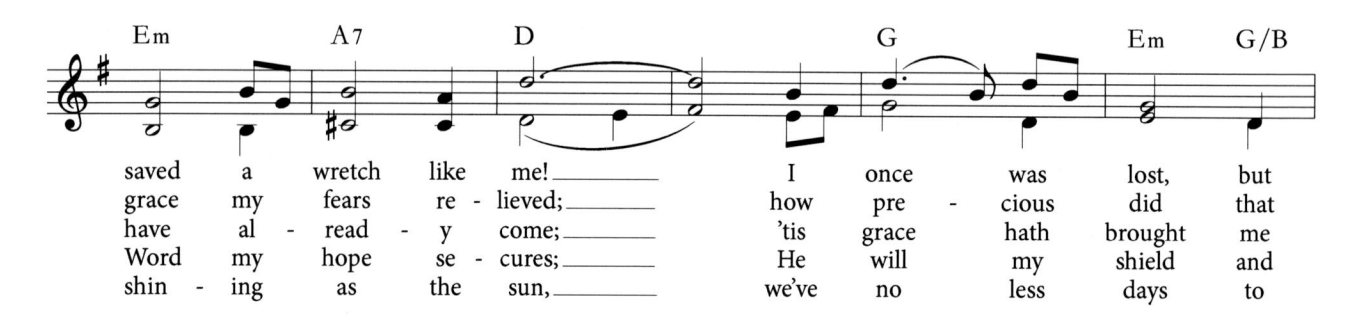

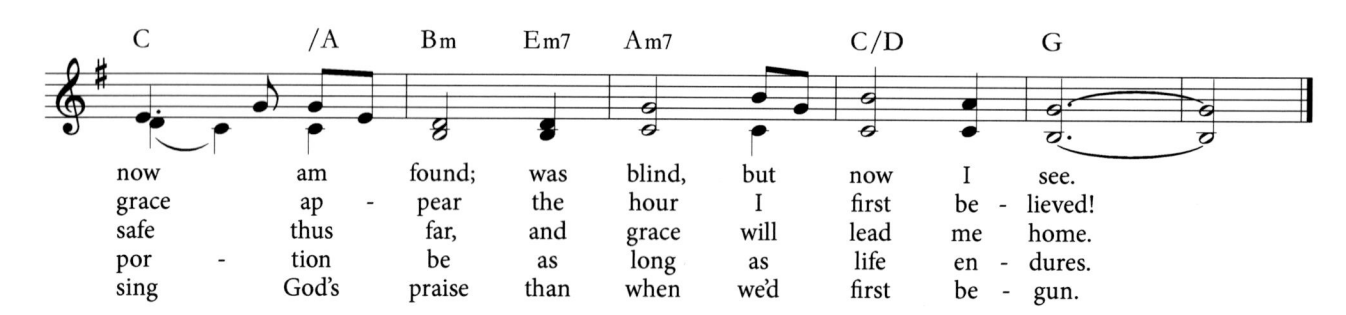

1. A-maz-ing grace! how sweet the sound, that saved a wretch like me! I once was lost, but now am found; was blind, but now I see.
2. 'Twas grace that taught my heart to fear, and grace my fears re-lieved; how pre-cious did that grace ap-pear the hour I first be-lieved!
3. Through man-y dan-gers, toils, and snares, I have al-read-y come; 'tis grace hath brought me safe thus far, and grace will lead me home.
4. The Lord has prom-ised good to me; His Word my hope se-cures; He will my shield and por-tion be as long as life en-dures.
5. When we've been there ten thou-sand years, bright shin-ing as the sun, we've no less days to sing God's praise than when we'd first be-gun.

TEXT: John Newton, 1779 (st. 1-4); Anonymous, c. 1790 (st. 5)
MUSIC: William Walker, *Southern Harmony*, 1835

NEW BRITAIN
CM

Be Thou My Vision

*My flesh and my heart may fail, but God is the strength of
my heart and my portion forever. Psalm 73:26*

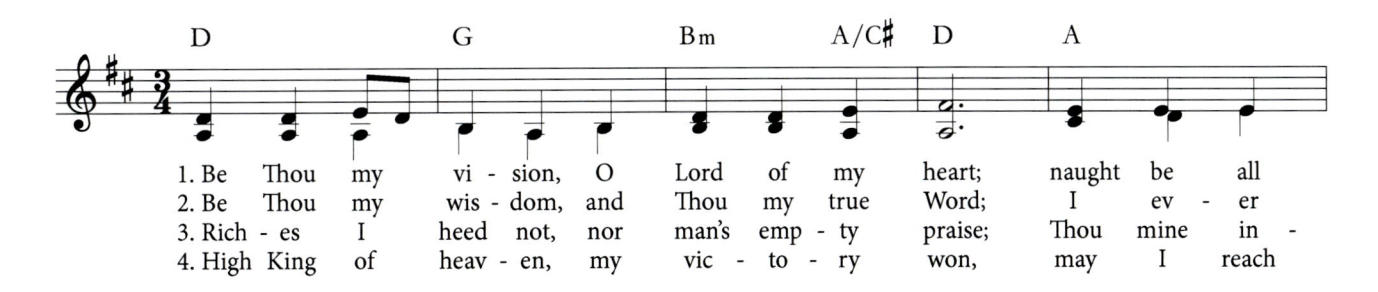

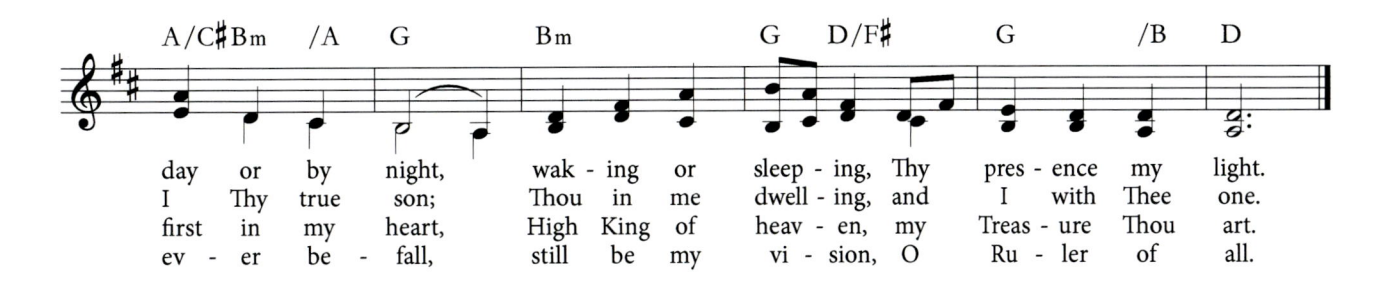

1. Be Thou my vision, O Lord of my heart; naught be all else to me, save that Thou art: Thou my best thought by day or by night, waking or sleeping, Thy presence my light.
2. Be Thou my wisdom, and Thou my true Word; I ever with Thee and Thou with me, Lord. Thou my great Father, I Thy true son; Thou in me dwelling, and I with Thee one.
3. Riches I heed not, nor man's empty praise; Thou mine inheritance, now and always: Thou and Thou only first in my heart, High King of heaven, my Treasure Thou art.
4. High King of heaven, my victory won, may I reach heaven's joys, O bright heaven's Sun! Heart of my own heart, whatever befall, still be my vision, O Ruler of all.

TEXT: 8th-century hymn, trans. Mary Elizabeth Byrne, vers. Eleanor Hull, 1912
MUSIC: Irish folk melody

SLANE
10.10.10.10

Christ the Lord Is Risen Today

*"Why do you seek the living One among the dead?
He is not here, but He has risen!" Luke 24:4-5*

1. Christ the Lord is ris'n to-day, Al - le - lu - ia!
2. Lives a - gain, our glo - rious King. Al - le - lu - ia!
3. Love's re - deem - ing work is done. Al - le - lu - ia!
4. Soar we now where Christ has led. Al - le - lu - ia!

Sons of men and an - gels say: Al - le - lu - ia!
Where, O death, is now thy sting? Al - le - lu - ia!
Fought the fight, the bat - tle won. Al - le - lu - ia!
Fol - l'wing our ex - alt - ed Head. Al - le - lu - ia!

Raise your joys and tri - umphs high. Al - le - lu - ia!
Dy - ing once, He all doth save. Al - le - lu - ia!
Death in vain for - bids Him rise. Al - le - lu - ia!
Made like Him, like Him we rise. Al - le - lu - ia!

Sing, ye heav'ns, and earth re - ply: Al - le - lu - ia!
Where thy vic - to - ry, O grave? Al - le - lu - ia!
Christ has o - pened par - a - dise. Al - le - lu - ia!
Ours the cross, the grave, the skies. Al - le - lu - ia!

TEXT: Charles Wesley, 1739
MUSIC: *Lyra Davidica*, 1708

EASTER HYMN
77.77 with alleluias

Come, Christians, Join to Sing

*I have proclaimed glad tidings of righteousness in the great congregation; behold,
I will not restrain my lips, O Lord! Psalm 40:9*

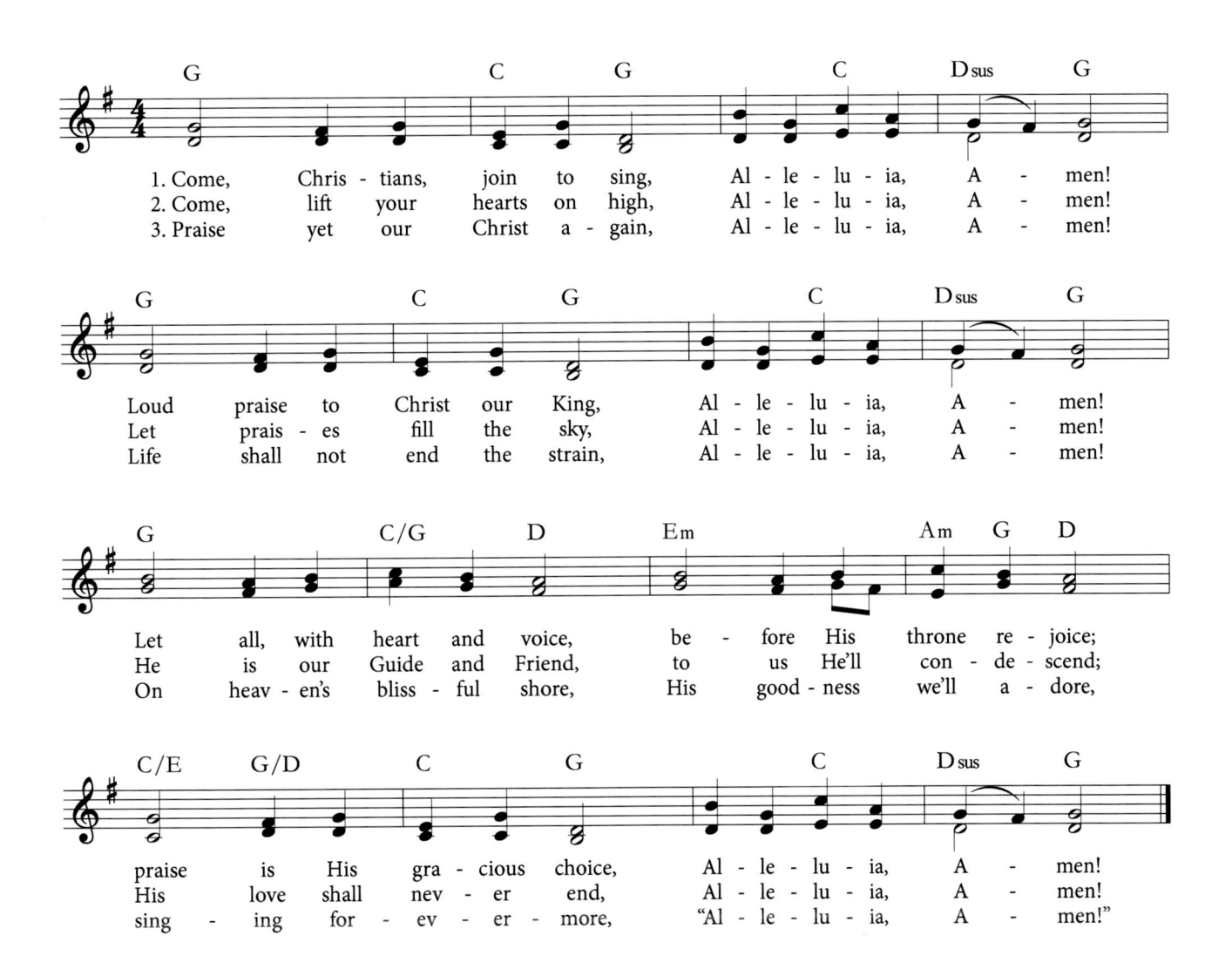

1. Come, Christians, join to sing, Alleluia, Amen!
   Loud praise to Christ our King, Alleluia, Amen!
   Let all, with heart and voice, before His throne rejoice;
   praise is His gracious choice, Alleluia, Amen!

2. Come, lift your hearts on high, Alleluia, Amen!
   Let praises fill the sky, Alleluia, Amen!
   He is our Guide and Friend, to us He'll condescend;
   His love shall never end, Alleluia, Amen!

3. Praise yet our Christ again, Alleluia, Amen!
   Life shall not end the strain, Alleluia, Amen!
   On heaven's blissful shore, His goodness we'll adore,
   singing forevermore, "Alleluia, Amen!"

TEXT: Christian Bateman, 1843
MUSIC: Spanish melody

MADRID
66.66 D

Come, My Soul, with Every Care

"Be anxious for nothing, but in everything by prayer and supplication, with thanksgiving, let your requests be made known to God." Philippians 4:6

Come my soul, with ev - 'ry care; Je - sus loves to an - swer prayer. He Him-
With my bur - den I be - gin: Lord, re - move this load of sin; Let Your
Lord, I am a pil - grim here, let Your love my spir - it cheer. As my

self bids you to pray and will nev - er turn a - way. You are
blood, for sin - ners spilt, set my con - science free from guilt. With Your
guide, my guard, my friend, lead me to my jour - ney's end. Show me

com - ing to a king, large pe - ti - tions with you bring, For His
rest to me im - part; take pos - ses - sion of my heart. There Your
what I am to do; Ev - 'ry hour my strength re - new. *I would

grace and pow'r are such, none can ev - er ask too much.
blood - bought right main - tain and with - out a ri - val reign.
have Your will, not mine; for it's per - fect, good, and kind.

TEXT: John Newton, alt.*
MUSIC: Fred and Ruth Coleman

Music 2010 Fred and Ruth Coleman. All rights reserved.

KEESEE
7.7.7.7.D

Crown Him With Many Crowns

His eyes are a flame of fire, and on His head are many diadems... Revelation 19:12

1. Crown Him with many crowns, the Lamb upon His throne;
2. Crown Him the Lord of love; behold His hands and side,
3. Crown Him the Lord of life, who triumphed o'er the grave,
4. Crown Him the Lord of Heav'n, one with the Father known;

hark, how the heav'nly anthem drowns all music but its own!
rich wounds, yet visible above, in beauty glorified.
and rose victorious in the strife for those He came to save.
One with the Spirit through Him giv'n from His eternal throne.

Awake, my soul, and sing of Him who died for thee,
No angel in the sky can fully bear that sight,
His glories now we sing, who died and rose on high,
To You be endless praise, For You have died for me;

and hail Him as thy matchless King through all eternity.
but downward bends his burning eye at mysteries so bright.
who died eternal life to bring, and lives that death may die.
Your praise and glory shall not fail throughout eternity!

TEXT: Matthew Bridges, 1852, and Godfrey Thring, 1874
MUSIC: George Elvey, 1868

DIADEMATA
SMD

Fairest Lord Jesus

You are fairer than the sons of men... therefore God has blessed You forever. Psalm 45:2

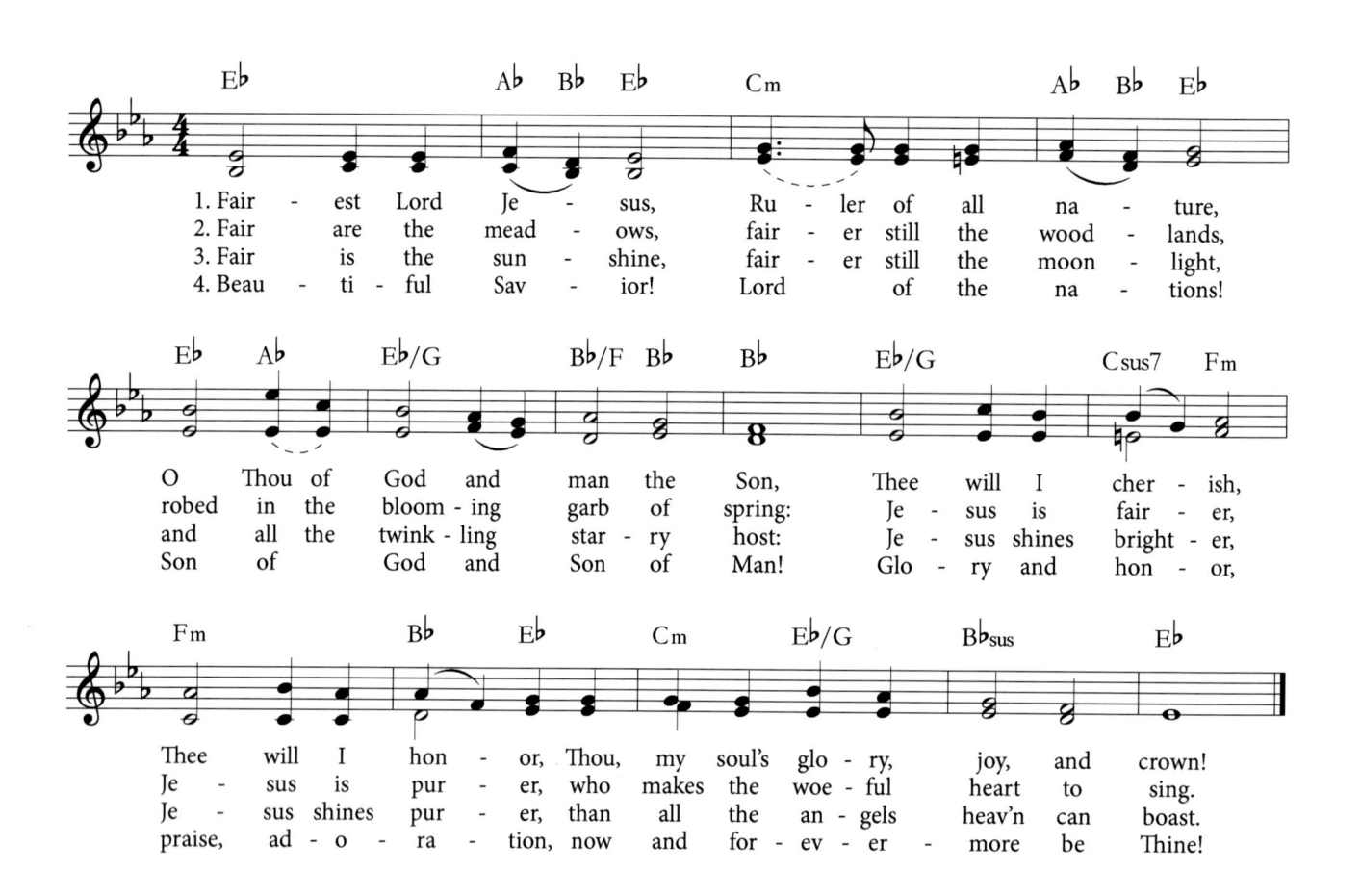

1. Fair-est Lord Je-sus, Ru-ler of all na-ture,
O Thou of God and man the Son,
Thee will I cher-ish,
Thee will I hon-or, Thou, my soul's glo-ry, joy, and crown!

2. Fair are the mead-ows, fair-er still the wood-lands,
robed in the bloom-ing garb of spring:
Je-sus is fair-er,
Je-sus is pur-er, who makes the woe-ful heart to sing.

3. Fair is the sun-shine, fair-er still the moon-light,
and all the twink-ling star-ry host:
Je-sus shines bright-er,
Je-sus shines pur-er, than all the an-gels heav'n can boast.

4. Beau-ti-ful Sav-ior! Lord of the na-tions!
Son of God and Son of Man!
Glo-ry and hon-or,
praise, ad-o-ra-tion, now and for-ev-er-more be Thine!

TEXT: *Muenster Gesangbuch*, 1677
MUSIC: Silesian folk melody, *Schleische Volkslieder*, 1842

CRUSADERS' HYMN
56.85.58

God Moves in a Mysterious Way

Oh, the depth of the riches both of the wisdom and knowledge of God! How unsearchable are His judgments and unfathomable His ways! Romans 11:33

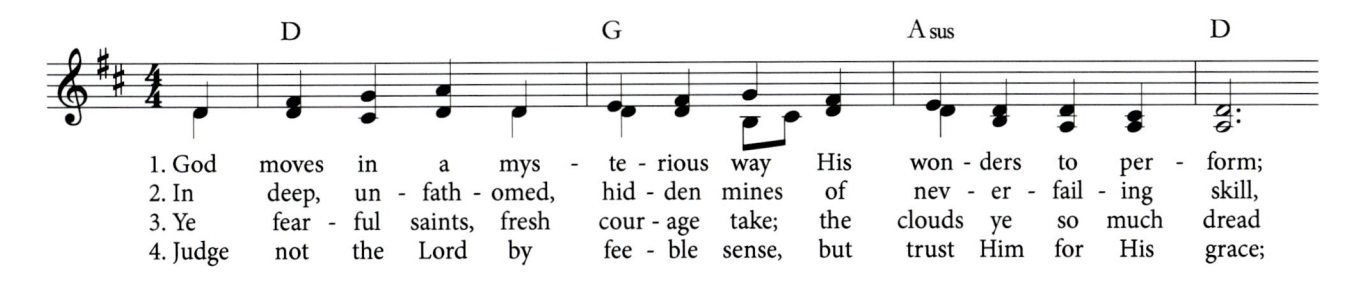

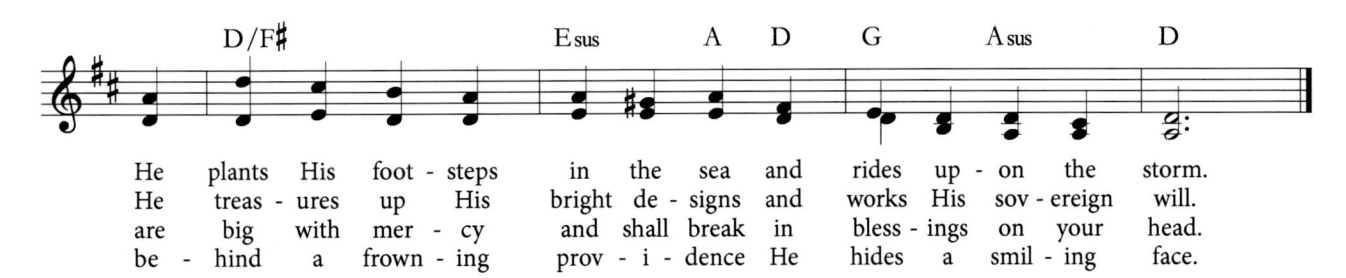

1. God moves in a mysterious way His wonders to perform;
   He plants His footsteps in the sea and rides upon the storm.
2. In deep, unfathomed, hidden mines of never-failing skill,
   He treasures up His bright designs and works His sovereign will.
3. Ye fearful saints, fresh courage take; the clouds ye so much dread
   are big with mercy and shall break in blessings on your head.
4. Judge not the Lord by feeble sense, but trust Him for His grace;
   behind a frowning providence He hides a smiling face.

5. His purposes will ripen fast,
   unfolding every hour;
   the bud may have a bitter taste,
   but sweet will be the flower.

6. Blind unbelief is sure to err,
   and scan His work in vain;
   God is His own interpreter,
   and He will make it plain.

TEXT: William Cowper, 1774
MUSIC: *Scottish Psalter*, 1615

DUNDEE
CM

What Does It Cost to Follow Jesus?

(optional partner song with "I Have Decided to Follow Jesus")

Sing with repeat of last stanza.

*I have decided to follow Jesus, I have decided to follow Jesus, I have decided to follow Jesus— no turning back, no turning back.

1. What does it cost to follow Jesus? What is the price Jesus, to do His will? How can you be His true disciple, and through your life His call fulfill?

2. The price is high to follow Jesus, So count the cost before you start. Take up your cross, and follow Jesus, with mind, and strength, with soul, and heart.

3. I'll count the cost to follow Jesus. Forsaking all, I'll heed His call. I'll take my cross and follow Jesus, I'll give to Christ my all in all.

TEXT: from Luke 14:25-35, Michael S. Bryson
MUSIC: Michael S. Bryson

* "I Have Decided to Follow Jesus" - words: anonymous, music: Indian folk tune [ASSAM]

© 2021 Celebrating Grace, Inc., Macon, GA
www.celebrating-grace.com All rights reserved.
Used by permission.

I Sing the Mighty Power of God

*In six days the L<small>ORD</small> made heaven and earth,
the sea, and all that is in them... Exodus 20:11*

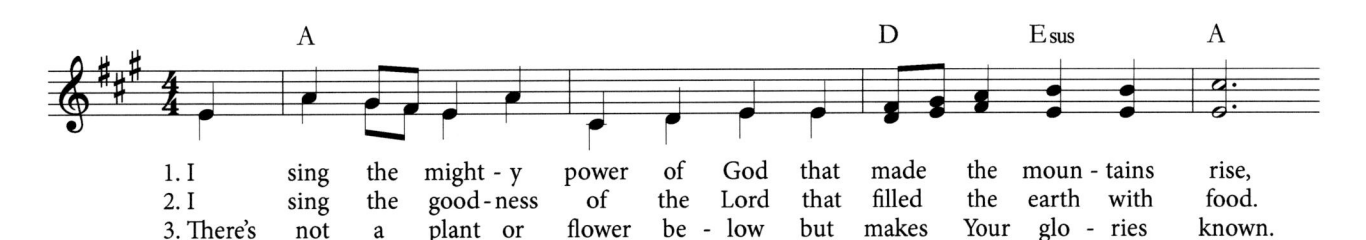

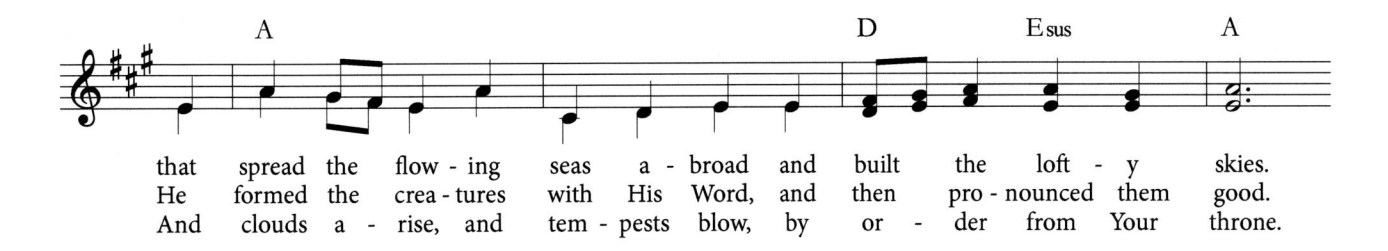

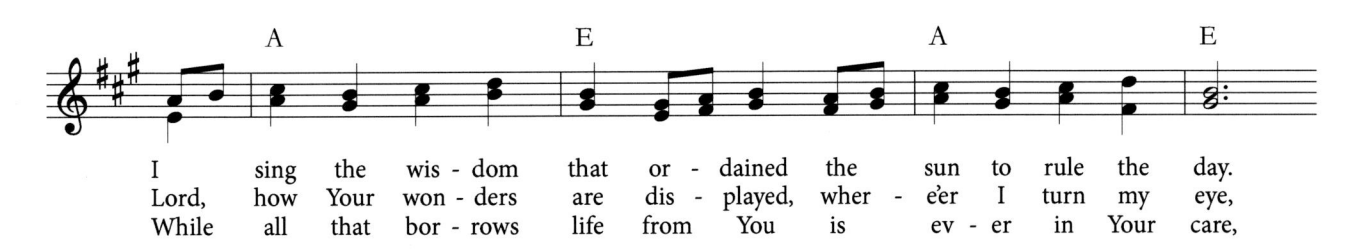

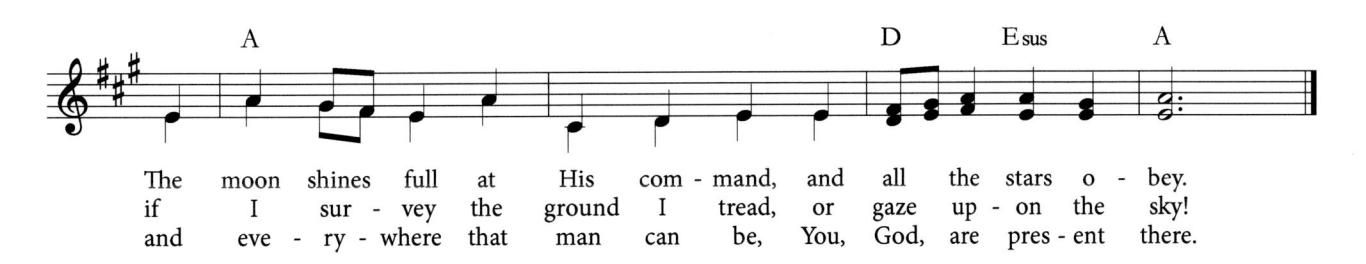

1. I sing the mighty power of God that made the mountains rise,
that spread the flowing seas abroad and built the lofty skies.
I sing the wisdom that ordained the sun to rule the day.
The moon shines full at His command, and all the stars obey.

2. I sing the goodness of the Lord that filled the earth with food.
He formed the creatures with His Word, and then pronounced them good.
Lord, how Your wonders are displayed, where-e'er I turn my eye,
if I survey the ground I tread, or gaze upon the sky!

3. There's not a plant or flower below but makes Your glories known.
And clouds arise, and tempests blow, by order from Your throne.
While all that borrows life from You is ever in Your care,
and everywhere that man can be, You, God, are present there.

TEXT: Isaac Watts, 1715, alt.
MUSIC: *Gesangbuch der Herzogl*, 1784, alt.

ELLACOMBE
CMD

Jesus Shall Reign

May He come down like rain upon the mown grass, like showers that water the earth. In His days may the righteous flourish, and abundance of peace till the moon is no more. Psalm 72:6-7

1. Je-sus shall reign wher-e'er the sun does its suc-ces-sive journeys run; His king-dom spread from shore to shore, till moons shall wax and wane no more.
2. Peo-ple and realms of eve-ry tongue dwell on His love with sweet-est song, and in-fant voic-es shall pro-claim their earth-ly bless-ings on His name.
3. Let eve-ry crea-ture rise and bring their grate-ful hon-ors to our King. An-gels de-scend with songs a-gain, and earth re-peat the loud "A-men!"

He shall reign in glo-ry, crowned with grace and might. Bless His name, and praise the sov-ereign King. He shall reign for-ev-er with His cho-sen bride; all the earth shall sing that Je-sus is the King!

TEXT: Isaac Watts, 1719, alt.; and Ryan Foglesong
MUSIC: John Hatton, 1793, and Ryan Foglesong

DUKE STREET
LM with chorus

May the Mind of Christ, My Savior

Have this attitude in yourselves which was also in Christ Jesus... Philippians 2:5

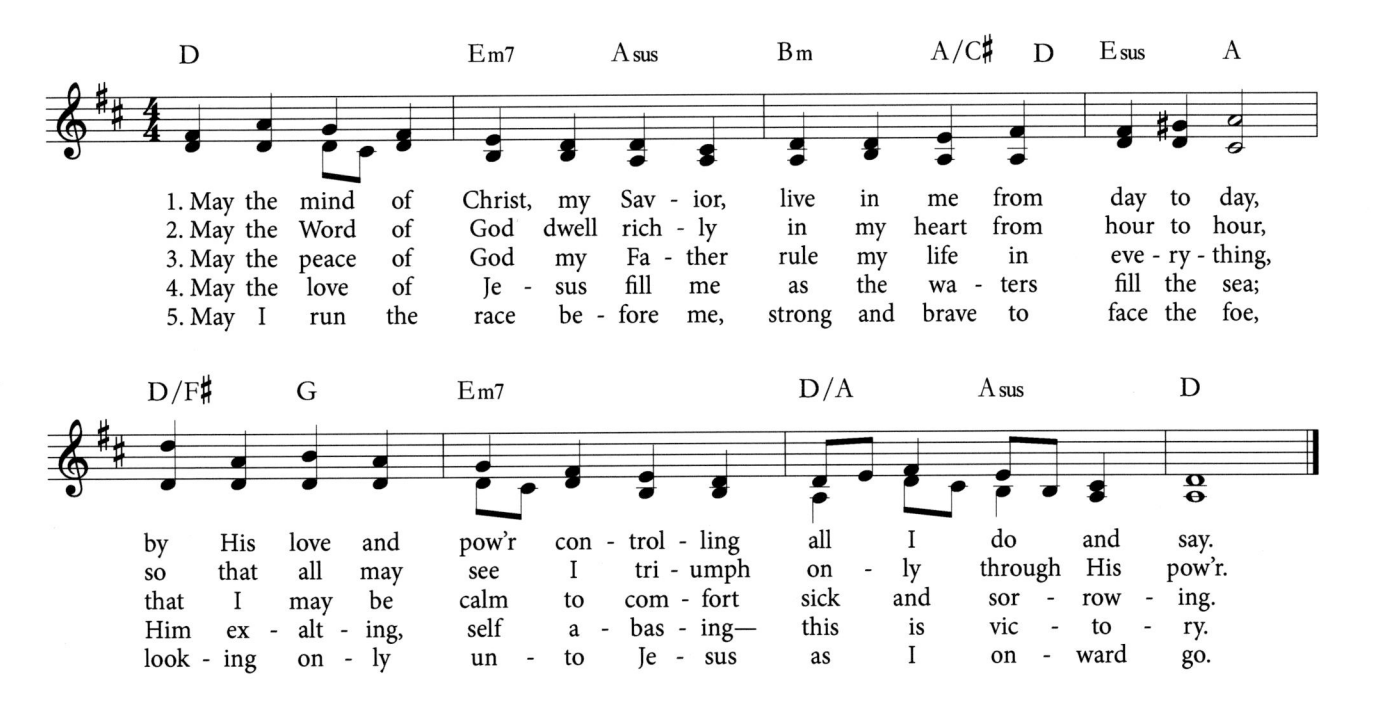

1. May the mind of Christ, my Savior, live in me from day to day,
by His love and pow'r controlling all I do and say.

2. May the Word of God dwell richly in my heart from hour to hour,
so that all may see I triumph only through His pow'r.

3. May the peace of God my Father rule my life in everything,
that I may be calm to comfort sick and sorrowing.

4. May the love of Jesus fill me as the waters fill the sea;
Him exalting, self abasing— this is victory.

5. May I run the race before me, strong and brave to face the foe,
looking only unto Jesus as I onward go.

TEXT: Kate B. Wilkinson, 1925
MUSIC: A. Cyril Barham-Gould, 1925

ST. LEONARDS
87.85

O Worship the King

*The Lord is my rock and my fortress and my deliverer, my God, my rock, in whom
I take refuge; my shield and the horn of my salvation, my stronghold. Psalm 18:2*

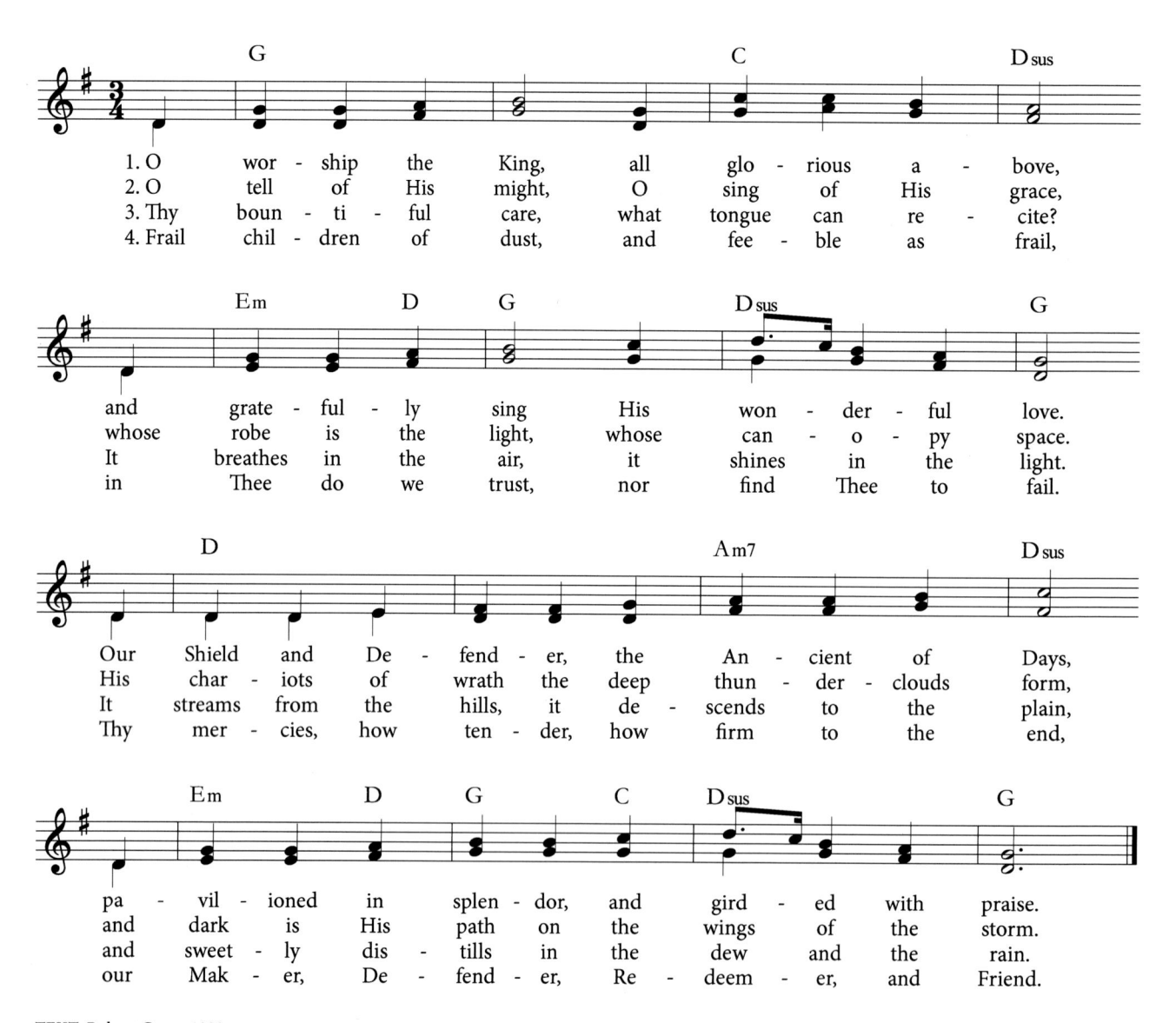

1. O worship the King, all glorious above,
   and gratefully sing His wonderful love.
   Our Shield and Defender, the Ancient of Days,
   pavilioned in splendor, and girded with praise.

2. O tell of His might, O sing of His grace,
   whose robe is the light, whose canopy space.
   His chariots of wrath the deep thunderclouds form,
   and dark is His path on the wings of the storm.

3. Thy bountiful care, what tongue can recite?
   It breathes in the air, it shines in the light.
   It streams from the hills, it descends to the plain,
   and sweetly distills in the dew and the rain.

4. Frail children of dust, and feeble as frail,
   in Thee do we trust, nor find Thee to fail.
   Thy mercies, how tender, how firm to the end,
   our Maker, Defender, Redeemer, and Friend.

TEXT: Robert Grant, 1833
MUSIC: W. Gardiner's *Sacred Melodies*, 1815; attr. Johann Michael Haydn

LYONS
10.10.11.11

The King of Love My Shepherd Is

*Surely goodness and mercy shall follow me all the days of my life,
and I shall dwell in the house of the L<small>ORD</small> forever. Psalm 23:6*

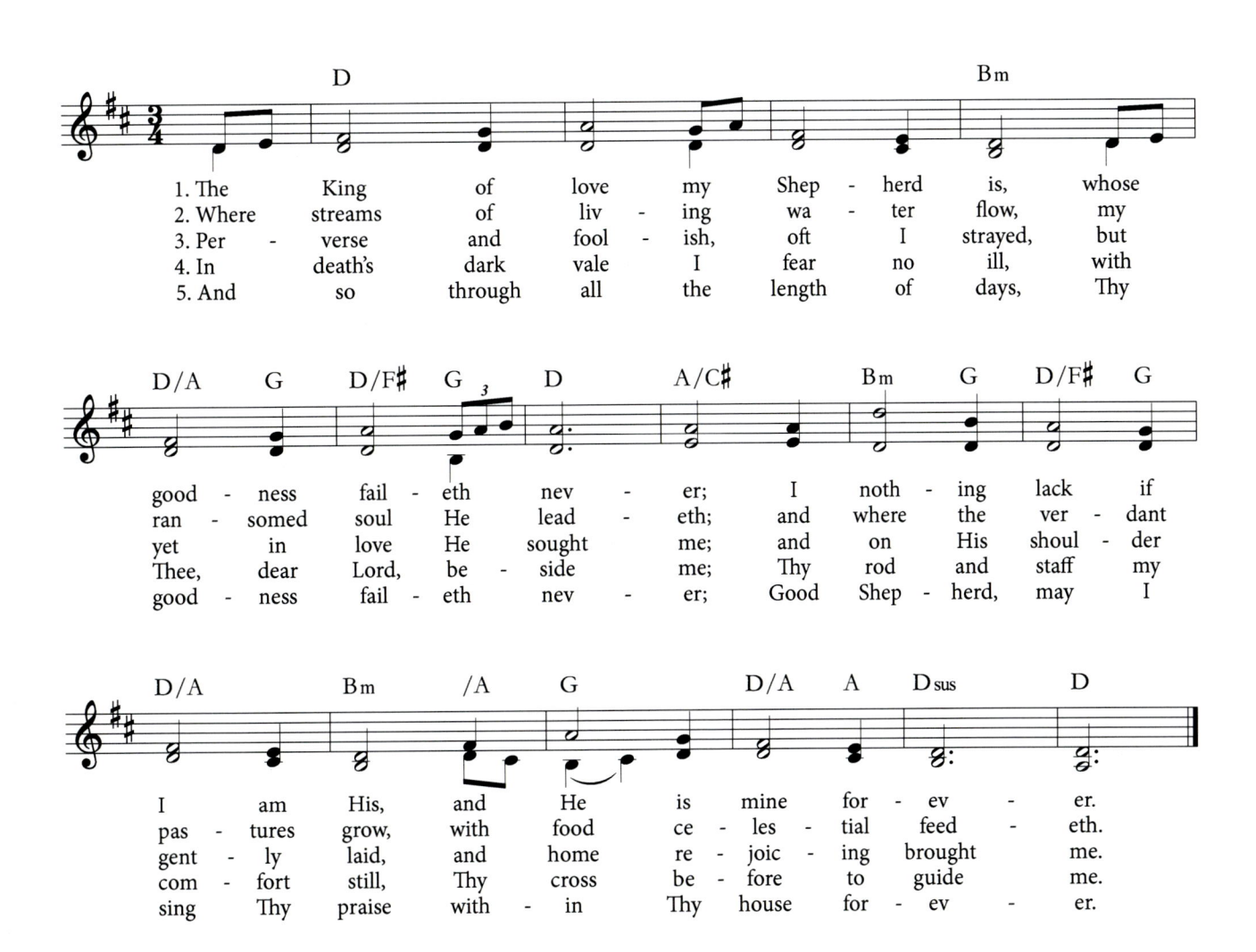

1. The King of love my Shepherd is, whose goodness faileth never; I nothing lack if I am His, and He is mine forever.
2. Where streams of living water flow, my ransomed soul He leadeth; and where the verdant pastures grow, with food celestial feedeth.
3. Perverse and foolish, oft I strayed, but yet in love He sought me; and on His shoulder gently laid, and home rejoicing brought me.
4. In death's dark vale I fear no ill, with Thee, dear Lord, beside me; Thy rod and staff my comfort still, Thy cross before to guide me.
5. And so through all the length of days, Thy goodness faileth never; Good Shepherd, may I sing Thy praise within Thy house forever.

TEXT: Henry Williams Baker, 1868
MUSIC: Irish melody, harmonized in *The English Hymnal*, 1906

ST. COLUMBA
87.87

109

This Is My Father's World

The earth is the Lord's, and all it contains;
the world, and those who dwell in it. Psalm 24:1

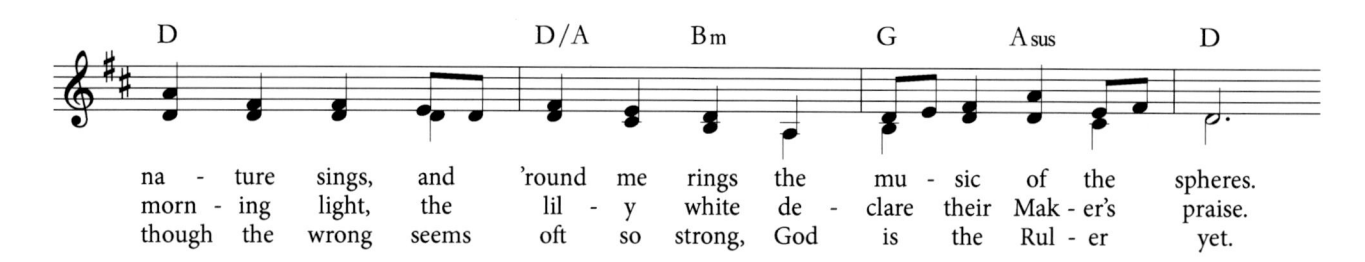

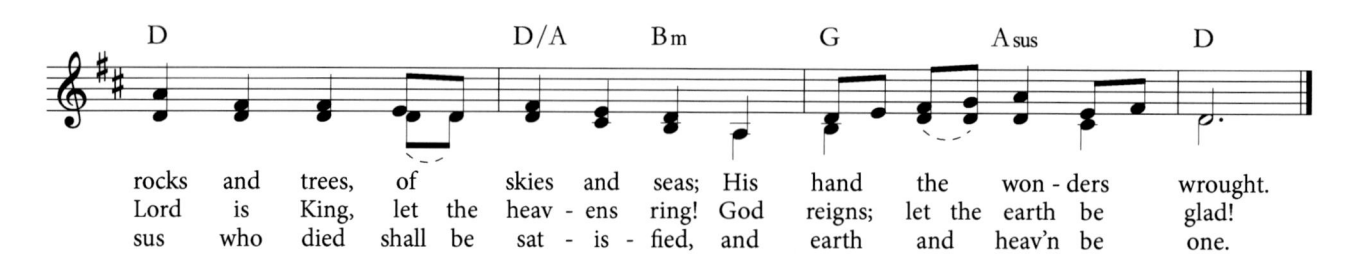

1. This is my Father's world, and to my listening ears all nature sings, and 'round me rings the music of the spheres. This is my Father's world; I rest me in the thought of rocks and trees, of skies and seas; His hand the wonders wrought.

2. This is my Father's world; the birds their carols raise; the morning light, the lily white declare their Maker's praise. This is my Father's world; why should my heart be sad? The Lord is King, let the heavens ring! God reigns; let the earth be glad!

3. This is my Father's world; oh, let me not forget that though the wrong seems oft so strong, God is the Ruler yet. This is my Father's world, the battle is not done; Jesus who died shall be satisfied, and earth and heav'n be one.

TEXT: Maltbie D. Babcock, 1901
MUSIC: Franklin L. Sheppard, 1915

TERRA BEATA
SMD

Trust and Obey

"If you keep My commandments, you will abide in My love... These things I have spoken to you so that My joy may be in you, and that your joy may be made full." John 15:10-11

1. When we walk with the Lord in the light of His Word, what a glory He sheds on our way! While we do His good will, He abides with us still, and with all who will trust and o-bey.
2. Not a bur-den we bear, not a sor-row we share, but our toil He doth rich-ly re-pay; not a grief or a loss, not a frown or a cross, but is blessed if we trust and o-bey.
3. But we nev-er can prove the de-lights of His love, un-til all on the al-tar we lay; for the fa-vor He shows and the joy He be-stows are for those who will trust and o-bey.
4. Then in fel-low-ship sweet we will sit at His feet, or we'll walk by His side in the way; what He says we will do, where He sends we will go— nev-er fear, on-ly trust and o-bey.

Refrain:
Trust and o-bey, for there's no oth-er way to be hap-py in Je-sus, but to trust and o-bey.

TEXT: John H. Sammis, 1887
MUSIC: Daniel B. Towner, 1887

TRUST AND OBEY

Index

Studies

Study 1	Following Jesus Means Being a Servant	1
Study 2	True Disciples Follow and Obey	3
Study 3	Jesus' Fame Grows	5
Study 4	First Things First	7
Study 5	Seeing Jesus, Not Rules: Part 1/3 "Forgiver"	9
Study 6	Seeing Jesus, Not Rules: Part 2 / 3 "Eating"	11
Study 7	Seeing Jesus, Not Rules: Part 3/3 "Sabbath"	13
Study 8	Conflict and Desires	15
Study 9	Choosing Sides	17
Study 10	Jesus' Teaching: 1/3 "Hidden in Plain Sight"	19
Study 11	Jesus' Teaching: 2 /3 "Listen Carefully"	21
Study 12	Jesus' Teaching: 3/3 "Meager to Mighty"	23
Study 13	Seeing Jesus: 1 / 4 "Power Over Creation"	25
Study 14	Seeing Jesus: 2 / 4 "Power Over Demons"	27
Study 15	Seeing Jesus: 3 / 4 "Power Over Sickness"	29
Study 16	Seeing Jesus: 4 / 4 "Power Over Death"	31
Study 17	Commitment to Jesus	33
Study 18	Bread & Water	35
Study 19	Unwelcome at Home	37
Study 20	Wash Up for Supper	39
Study 21	Jesus Preaches to Gentiles	41
Study 22	Second Helpings	43
Study 23	Missing the Point	45
Study 24	Seeing Clearly	47
Study 25	High Prices	49
Study 26	Jesus Reveals His Glory	51
Study 27	Divine Help	53
Study 28	Jesus Teaches: 1/5 "On Discipleship"	55
Study 29	Jesus Teaches: 2/5 "On Family"	57
Study 30	Jesus Teaches: 3/5 "On Wealth"	59
Study 31	Jesus Teaches: 4/5 "On Humility"	61
Study 32	Jesus Teaches: 5/5 "On Genuine Faith"	63
Study 33	Jesus' Authority: 1/5 "The Temple"	65
Study 34	Jesus' Authority: 2/5 "Rejection"	67
Study 35	Jesus' Authority: 3/5 "Taxes & Eternity"	69
Study 36	Jesus' Authority: 4/5 "Greatest Command"	71
Study 37	Jesus' Authority: 5/5 "Revealing the Heart"	73
Study 38	Signs of the End Times	75
Study 39	Be Vigilant	77
Study 40	Anointed Lamb	79
Study 41	The Last Passover Lamb	81
Study 42	Prayer & Betrayal in Gethsemane	83
Study 43	The Jewish Trial	85
Study 44	The Roman Trial	87
Study 45	God's Plan: the Crucifixion of Christ	89
Study 46	Being Jesus' Disciple	91
Study 47	Resurrection!	93

Hymns

All Creatures of our God and King	95
Amazing Grace	96
Be Thou My Vision	97
Christ the Lord Is Risen Today	98
Come, Christians, Join to Sing	99
Come, My Soul, with Every Care	100
Crown Him with Many Crowns	101
Fairest Lord Jesus	102
God Moves in a Mysterious Way	103
I Sing the Mighty Power of God	105
Jesus Shall Reign	106
May the Mind of Christ, My Savior	107
O Worship the King	108
The King of Love My Shepherd Is	109
This Is My Father's World	110
Trust and Obey	111
What Does It Cost to Follow Jesus	104